The PADRE of ISLETA

The PADRE of ISLETA
Facsimile of 1940 Edition

by
Julia Keleher and Elsie Ruth Chant

New Foreword
by
Michael L. Keleher

SANTA FE

New Material © 2009 by Sunstone Press. All Rights Reserved.

No part of this book may be reproduced in any form or by any electronic or mechanical means including information storage and retrieval systems without permission in writing from the publisher, except by a reviewer who may quote brief passages in a review.

Sunstone books may be purchased for educational, business, or sales promotional use. For information please write: Special Markets Department, Sunstone Press, P.O. Box 2321, Santa Fe, New Mexico 87504-2321.

Library of Congress Cataloging-in-Publication Data

Keleher, Julia.
 The padre of Isleta / by Julia Keleher and Elsie Ruth Chant ; new foreword by Michael L. Keleher. -- Facsim. of 1940 ed.
   p. cm. -- (Southwest heritage series)
 Originally published: Santa Fe, N.M. : Rydal Press, 1940. With new foreword.
 Includes bibliographical references and index.
 ISBN 978-0-86534-714-4 (softcovers : alk. paper)
 1. Docher, Anton, d. 1928. 2. Isleta Indians--Missions--New Mexico--Isleta Pueblo. 3. Priests--New Mexico--Isleta Pueblo--Biography. 4. Missionaries--New Mexico --Isleta Pueblo--Biography. 5. Catholic Church--Missions--New Mexico--Isleta Pueblo--Histoyr. 6. Isleta Pueblo (N.M.)--Religious life and customs.
 7. Isleta Pueblo (N.M.)--Social lfie and customs. I. Chant, Elsie Ruth. II. Title.
 E99.I8D635 2009
 282.092--dc22
 [B]
                        2009006804

WWW.SUNSTONEPRESS.COM
SUNSTONE PRESS / POST OFFICE BOX 2321 / SANTA FE, NM 87504-2321 /USA
(505) 988-4418 / ORDERS ONLY (800) 243-5644 / FAX (505) 988-1025

The Southwest Heritage Series is dedicated to Jody Ellis and Marcia Muth Miller, the founders of Sunstone Press, whose original purpose and vision continues to inspire and motivate our publications.

CONTENTS

THE SOUTHWEST HERITAGE SERIES / I

FOREWORD TO THIS EDITION / II

FACSIMILE OF 1940 EDITION / III

I

THE SOUTHWEST HERITAGE SERIES

"The past is not dead. In fact, it's not even past."
—William Faulkner, *Requiem for a Nun*

The history of the United States is written in hundreds of regional histories and literary works. Those letters, essays, memoirs, biographies and even collections of fiction are often first-hand accounts by people who wanted to memorialize an event, a person or simply record for posterity the concerns and issues of the times. Many of these accounts have been lost, destroyed or overlooked. Some are in private or public collections but deemed to be in too fragile condition to permit handling by contemporary readers and researchers.

However, now with the application of twenty-first century technology, nineteenth and twentieth century material can be reprinted and made accessible to the general public. These early writings are the DNA of our history and culture and are essential to understanding the present in terms of the past.

The Southwest Heritage Series is a form of literary preservation. Heritage by definition implies legacy and these early works are our legacy from those who have gone before us. To properly present and preserve that legacy, no changes in style or contents have been made. The material reprinted stands on its own as it first appeared. The point of view is that of the author and the era in which he or she lived. We would not expect photographs of people from the past to be re-imaged with modern clothes, hair styles and backgrounds. We should not, therefore, expect their ideas and personal philosophies to reflect our modern concepts.

Remember, reading their words and sharing their thoughts is a passport back into understanding how the past was shaped and how it influenced today's world.

Our hope is that new access to these older books will provide readers with a challenging and exciting experience.

Julia Keleher with Michael (left) and William Keleher.
Photograph from the William A. Keleher Pictorial Collection (PICT 000-742-0996),
courtesy of Center for Southwest Research, University Libraries, University of New Mexico.

II

FOREWORD TO THIS EDITION
by
Michael L. Keleher

Julia M. Keleher (May 30, 1894 – November 21, 1980) and Elsie Ruth Chant (June 30, 1902 – October 2, 1994) wrote *The Padre of Isleta* while they were with the English Department at the University of New Mexico. When the book was first published in 1940 by the Rydal Press, Santa Fe, New Mexico, I was six years old. Even so, I have vague memories of my father and Aunt Julia discussing the story of Father Anton Docher, the Catholic priest who served Isleta Pueblo for some 32 years. He arrived in Isleta December 28, 1891.

Julia was a member and Professor in the English Department from 1931 to her retirement in 1959. She never married, and lived with her sister Katherine Keleher, who taught for many years at the Albuquerque High School. They were both interesting and accomplished women, but different in a number of ways. Aunt Julia was professional, a reader and a writer. She edited each of her brother, William A. Keleher's books. I recall him saying that others might have some criticism, even an editor or publisher, but if Julia said the book was in good form, it was acceptable to him, and no changes would be made. Katherine Keleher was athletic and energetic, played golf, and was action oriented. They were very close, made a good combination of caring aunts for their nephews, of which I was one.

Elsie Ruth Chant married Lloyd Chant a successful electrical contractor and raised two children, George Ashley Chant of Albuquerque, and Julia Jane Chant Alford of Las Cruces.

The story of Father Docher was well worth writing. But the *Padre of Isleta* isn't just about him. Weaved into this book are accounts of "sun, silence and adobe," stories of the pueblo and its people, and stories of Father Docher's visits with Charles Fletcher Lummis and Adolph Bandelier, as well as the legend of the early Franciscan Padre Padilla whose casket mysteriously raised and created a tapping noise near the church sanctuary.

III

FACSIMILE OF 1940 EDITION

The Padre of Isleta

Julia Keleher and Elsie Ruth Chant

The Rydal Press
SANTA FE · NEW MEXICO

Father Docher walks in his garden at Isleta, enjoying the shade of the trees he planted.

Copyright 1940 by Julia Keleher and Elsie Ruth Chant
Printed in the U.S.A. by The Rydal Press

To Our Mothers

Acknowledgments

MANY friends have helped us in writing this book. We wish to express our thanks to all those who contributed facts, legends, or personal reminiscences concerning the Pueblo of Isleta, and the lives of Father Docher, Charles Lummis, and Adolphe Bandelier. We are especially indebted to the following for valuable information: Reverend Henry Pouget of Lenox, Iowa, a fellow-countryman, and life-long friend of Father Dochers; Reverend Jules N. Stoffel, personal friend of Father Dochers, also; Reverend Jules Hartmann, until recently resident-priest at Isleta; Lolita Huning Pooler, whose parents' home in Los Lunas was a gathering place of scholars and missionaries, and where Father Docher, Charles Lummis, and Adolphe Bandelier often met.

For helpful suggestions and encouragement in regard to the manuscript, we especially wish to thank Dr. George St. Clair, Dean Emeritus of the University of New Mexico, Dr. T. M. Pearce, Chairman of the English Department at the same University, Mr. Harry Hansen of New York City, and Professor James S. Wilson of the Bread Loaf School of English.

Although Father Docher lived at Isleta for thirty-four years and was identified in a vital way with individual and community life there, he left no memoirs. Many facts of his early life in France are not available; for these reasons no attempt was made at a complete biography of the padre who served in an Indian village where tradition governs the individual, where facts become legends, and legends become facts. In an attempt to personify Charles Lummis, and Adolphe Bandelier, we have quoted, or paraphrased in a few instances, their own words. This is true of quotations on pp. 1 and 2 of Chapter II. Adolphe Bandelier's version of Father Padilla is his own, and may be found in the *Catholic Quarterly Review* XV, No. 59, pp. 551-565.

Contents

	Introduction	
1	The Padre Comes to Isleta	17
2	Father Docher's First Caller	22
3	Kimo the Lion-Hearted	27
4	Los Lunas	30
5	The Legend of Father Padilla	37
6	Adolphe Bandelier Visits the Padre	41
7	An Ethnologist's Viewpoint	46
8	The Church and Legend	50
9	A Christening	54
10	The Feast of All Souls	58
11	El Padre Sargento	62
12	The Witch	67
13	El Santo Niño	71
14	Justice is Administered	77
15	Archbishop Chapelle is Welcomed	83
16	Charles Fletcher Lummis Returns to Isleta	88
17	The King and Queen of Belgium Visit Isleta	94
18	St. Rosalie	98
19	Father Docher in St. Joseph's Hospital	102
20	History and Legend	108

ILLUSTRATIONS

Father Docher Walks in His Garden
Frontispiece

Interior of Mission Church at Isleta
Page 16

View of Padre Docher's Residence
Page 32

Charles Fletcher Lummis
Page 40

Scene in Front of Isleta Church
Page 48

View of Isleta
Page 72

Ad. F. Bandelier in 1891
Page 88

Padre Docher Proudly Wearing Medals
Page 96

Introduction

THE Pueblo of Isleta is situated on the left bank of the Rio Grande, thirteen miles south of Albuquerque, N. M. It is one of the largest geographically, and one of the most populous of the Tiwa group of villages. The Isleta Reservation extends east and west from the Manzano Range to the Rio Puerco, a distance of thirty miles, and north and south along the Rio Grande nine miles. About 2,009 of its 180,000 acres are under cultivation. At the present time the population of the Pueblo numbers about 1,200. Tradition has it that it was once an island, hence the Spanish name, Isleta. Some believe that the site has been changed since the sixteenth century; others that the bed of the river has changed. The Tiwa name for the Pueblo is Shiahwibak, meaning "knife laid in the ground to play 'hwib'," a primitive game.

According to tradition, the people of the village "fled in terror, at the sight of the strange yellow beings" who came up from the south in 1540. Francisco Vasquez de Coronado, and his Conquistadores did not stop at Isleta, however, but pressed on in the search for gold, stopping to winter at Tiguex, near the present site of Bernalillo, N. M. Judging from Casteñeda, the chronicler of the Coronado expedition, Isleta was probably the southernmost village he refers to in reporting of "twelve villages lying in Tiguex, a province on the banks of a large swift river in a spacious valley two leagues wide, with a very high round, snow-covered mountain chain east of it."

According to the Benavides *Memorial*, published in Madrid in 1630, there was a Mission in Isleta in 1629. Quoting from his record, translated by Mrs. Edward E. Ayer, annotated by F. W. Hodge, and Charles Fletcher Lummis: "Proceeding up the same river (Rio del Norte) seven leagues, there commences the Teoas nation, with fifteen or sixteen pueblos in which there must be seven thousand souls, in a district of twelve or thirteen leagues, all baptized; with two monasteries, that is, the one of San Francisco de Sandia and that of San Antonia de la Isleta. At these there are schools of reading and writing, singing, and all play instruments; and the pupils are well taught in the Doctrine (*doctrinesados*) and with much care in the polite (or civilized, political) life. These two monasteries and churches are very costly and beautiful *curiosos* (thanks to the solicitousness and ardor of the Religious who founded them.) And all other pueblos have also their very beautiful churches."

The resident priest in the Mission of Isleta at this time may have been Fray Esteban de Perea because he arrived in New Mexico about that time. Fray Juan de Salas is given credit for the erection of the Convento, and church records indicate that Fray Francisco de la Concepcion was resident priest in the Pueblo in 1636.

Fact clarifies the history of the village in relation to the Pueblo Uprising of 1680. Woven with threads of black is a story of horror of the missions in New Mexico in that year, splotched with the blood of twenty-two missionaries, four hundred colonizers, the destruction of the widely separated Missions, and the ruin of Santa Fe. Isleta, however, did not take part in the rebellion because the Spanish settlers took refuge there as soon as possible after the revolt began. In fear of the reputed two thousand revolting Indians, these settlers together with the Isletans, fled to the South, and established a village, Ysleta del Sur close to what is now El Paso. Governor Otermin, in reporting that terrible flight from the capital at Santa Fe, wrote that when he arrived at Isleta he found the Mission in ruins, and the church being used for a stable.

Important historically is the date of 1709 in relation to Isleta because at that time the village was re-populated by scattered Tiwa tribes, and the Mission was rebuilt by Friar Juan de la Peña. The church is on the north side of the plaza around which the houses of the village are grouped. It is 110 feet by 27 feet, lighted by four high windows. The walls are four feet in thickness.

The village has up to the present time, maintained among the older people, manners and customs which were in practice when Castañeda described the manners and customs of the Tiguex Province four centuries ago.

J. K.
E. R. C.

The Padre of Isleta

Interior of the mission church at Isleta as it appeared during the years of Padre Docher's residence at the pueblo.

I

The Padre Comes to Isleta

OUT from the countless centuries which have flowed around Isleta, New Mexico, Time picks up the unrecorded threads of the past and weaves the story of the beginnings of life there. The myth tells of ancestors coming up from the center of the earth "in the bowels of which all men are created equal," and being led by divine beings to a low ridge of lava-flow east of the Rio Grande as the spot most suitable for a Tiwa Indian settlement.

Over the Creation myth, out of threads of legend, Time weaves another story of the origin of life in Isleta by ancestors who came down from the tops of the Sandia Mountains, and built houses of mud on a narrow neck of land cut by the river on its leisurely way to the Gulf of Mexico.

That the stream of life might flow on uninterruptedly on this "little island," the sound of the tom-tom beat out the Indian's religion of nature, a constant plea for new life—children, animals, crops. The pat of their feet beat down into the Earth-Mother the need for the growth of the seed; prayers ascended to the Sun-Father for the need for germination; arms upstretched, reaching, swinging down, bringing rainwater for all life in the earth-bowl. The men in the front rows, swinging their feet high and stamping the earth hard in their dancing, they the germ of life, the beginning; behind them the women, bare feet slow-moving, stolid and calm, they the earth, the slow growth of the germ cells.

Over this unblurred traditional pattern of Isleta life, History weaves the facts of Spanish conquest, and Indian submission, and over myth, legend, tradition and history, Christianity has woven a Cross.

To Isleta Pueblo, on December 28, 1891, rode a young missionary,

The Padre of Isleta

Father Anton Docher. As the darkness closed around him with a swift finality, he began to hum the Litany of the Saints to an improvised tune. There were so many saints on the long roster about whom he knew little that he always hesitated in asking their intercession on such occasions as this when there was danger of a man breaking his neck, or a horse its leg; rather, he counted on old friends such as St. Jude the Obscure, or St. Michael the Battler of Fallen Angels. The padre was tired. Taos, Santa Fe, Albuquerque lay behind him, but his destination was still several miles ahead in the gloom.

"Of course," remarked the Reverend P. Eguillon, Rector of St. Francis Cathedral at Santa Fe, as he gave the young priest final directions in regard to the location of Isleta, "the road is bad, but the sunset is always magnificent." But the Vicar-General had neglected to state, Father Docher reflected as he tightened his muffler, that the ruts in the road had probably been made by *caballeros* of long ago, and that after the steel-blue twilight blotted out the sunset beauty of a rose and lavender mountain wall, winds were swept from those snow-crested heights by demons who knifed their way through the valley unchallenged.

He finished the Litany of the Saints on a hopeful note, and out of the silence high above the cry of the wind, the padre seemed to hear the voices of others "who had passed that way"; prehistoric red man, conquistador, soldier of the Cross. For the first time since coming to New Mexico he felt the significance of becoming a part of such a heritage. He reverently saluted those whom he recognized in that kaleidoscopic procession of the ages as it imaginatively streamed by him on that river-road of timelessness and time; Coronado the great conqueror; Castañeda the first historian; Father Padilla, New Spain's first Christian martyr; Oñate the colonizer; Villagrá the poet; Benavides, Father Custodian of Missions; De Vargas the great re-conqueror—all on their way to destiny over ruts still apparent in the road. There would always be ruts in the road, the priest reflected, over which he would stumble. There would always be doubts, misapprehensions, fears. But there was always the New Mexico sunshine which he had noticed quickly dried the mud caked on boot or wagon wheel. There would always be prayer to help him over the difficulties of imparting the word of God to Indians,

The Padre Comes to Isleta

Spaniards, and Anglos, from the viewpoint of a French heritage.

"New Mexico's history is a pageant of legend and fact," Father Eguillon had told him. "A knowledge of the heritage of a people is necessary if one is to understand character moulded on ancient beliefs, on ingrained convictions, on prejudices, on superstitions. Missionaries must be resourceful men, those who do not indulge in the Simeon Stylites method of dependence on God." Both men had smiled, and the experienced churchman as he looked at the young missionary's firm chin, at the grey eyes with the twinkle never far away, realized that such indications of character and personality had been some of the deciding factors in Archbishop Salpointe's selection of the young Frenchman as resident priest at Isleta and surrounding Spanish villages.

"It will be your duty to keep the tangled strands of history and legends separated," the Vicar-General had added with his final blessing, "so that the design in the pattern of each life will show the Christian imprint. Facts can be learned, legends must be interpreted, for they reveal a way of life which has structure and substance from the perspective of the people who believe them." Then, as a parting thought, "It is with the imaginative features of an ancient civilization that one sometimes has difficulty," sighed the distinguished co-worker of the late Archbishop Lamy.

And now on this lonely stretch of wilderness, with nothing to break the flow of his thoughts but the dying winds and the far-off howl of a coyote, the padre found himself in entire agreement with the Vicar-General's analysis. For he suddenly became caught in a curious mesh of unreality bordered by an unexplainable golden glow spread against the darkness ahead of him, and he wondered if he were on the verge of another imaginative experience such as he had on the way down from Taos a week ago.

The memory would live with him always of how he had been awakened by the sound of marching feet. So near the measured tread had come that he had risen from his mountain bed lost in perplexity as to why a company of soldiers should be abroad in the night. He had waited tensely for the marchers to appear, straining his eyes in the dark to catch sight of them, but none had appeared. He had called, but only his own voice had broken the sound of hoofbeats faintly passing away in the canyon. With nerves taut and sleep

The Padre of Isleta

gone, he had rekindled his fire, rolled up his bedding and waited for the dawn to light his way down the gorge. In the golden reality of New Mexico sunshine he had convinced himself that the experience had been only a dream, until a Mexican sheepherder with whom he had shared his lunch had quietly asked him if he had heard the marchers. "Who are they?" the padre had asked. But the wizened and brown old man had only shaken his head and answered, "The souls of all those who have been killed in the Taos country. There are many who have heard them, but there is no one who has ever seen them." The priest now recalled how relieved he had felt, as he laughingly waved a *Dispensame por Dios* to the sheepherder, at leaving that part of New Mexico where people shut in by fortress-like mountains lived too much in the past.

In order to prove that the present phenomenon was merely a trick of vision, he tried blinking very hard several times, only to discover when he opened his eyes that the strange light had resolved into patterned formations. He had heard about apparitions called mirages, but those who had seen unusual sights in vast uninhabited stretches of the desert had explained to him that such illusions were caused by the rays of the sun.

The pinto quickened its pace at the padre's urging. Soon, blacker splotches of dark along the roadside became identified as houses, and then slowly the mystery dissolved into the traditional Spanish Christmas custom of which he had heard, that of decorating adobe houses with *luminarias* in honor and remembrance of the Christ Child. He gazed in awe at the scene, for he knew that the lights which threaded the little village with golden beauty were made by placing a white votive candle in a brown, sand-weighted paper sack at spaced intervals around the flat roofs. Not a phenomenon, but certainly magic, reflected the stranger, as he passed on into the dark.

The charm of the age-old custom which had brightened the remaining miles was completely snuffed out, however, by the sound of muffled drum-beats as the padre entered the plaza of the Indian village, and he was immediately projected into the reality of his future work there. As the rhythmic cadences of the tom-tom spread through the night the mystery of secret Indian ritual, Father Docher got off his horse and walked over to the church, looming to the north of the plaza. Secure on its foundations of history it seemed, and the

The Padre Comes to Isleta

uncertainty of his destiny brightened again as he remembered others who had come there to serve. Fray Esteban whom Benavides might have seen there in 1629, Fray de la Salas who erected the *Convento,* Fray Juan de la Peña who rebuilt the church after the original one had been destroyed by the Indian uprising in 1680.

Seeing a light to the left, he walked through the yard of the *Convento* and knocked at the door. *"Quien es?"* guardedly called the caretaker, as his wife drew back in alarm. *"Es el Padre Docher,"* came the answer. "Padre Docher," repeated the caretaker in reassuring tones to the woman, and then opened the door wide to receive him.

2

Father Docher's First Caller

"IT IS a land of sun, silence and adobe, Padre, and I think that you will like it."

Father Docher looked in amazement, in fact stared at a little man standing in the doorway of the room in the old *Convento* which he was trying to make habitable. It was a few mornings after his arrival in the pueblo, and at that particular moment he was in the process of cleaning out an old desk; the accumulation of the years was being dumped on the floor. Forgetting his manners, the priest stared again. The man couldn't possibly be an Indian; the voice lifted him completely out of that strata of civilization, and what he had just said made him—yes, a poet. "Sun, silence and adobe," Father Docher repeated. "Just what I have been thinking ever since I arrived in New Mexico, but what I would never in a thousand years be able to say.

"Come in," he said, after deciding that the caller was probably a chief who had been away to a Government school. Moccasins, corduroys, and a white shirt held in place by a wide red sash which matched in color a red tie certainly indicated something, or somebody.

"Yes, and it is also a land of *poco tiempo*," the man continued as he noticed the padre dusting off a chair with a bandana handkerchief. It was then, as the stranger stepped forward, that the padre noted the eagerness of the deep-set hazel eyes; a challenging sort of eagerness which the priest somehow liked, and accepted with a smile of welcome.

The new padre of Isleta waited for further enlightenment which was coming on a wave of enthusiasm. "My daughter was christened just yesterday, named 'Tur-be-se' which means 'Rainbow-of-the-Sun.' You would be very much interested in an Indian christening,

Father Docher's First Caller

I am sure. Ethnology is one of the most fascinating subjects in the world. Do you not agree?" But the padre's ethnological ignorance was lost on the caller as he hurried on to explain.

"Sometimes the ceremony is performed by the nearest neighbor, as in my case, who takes the child from the house at dawn on the third day after its birth, and names it after the first object that meets the eye after the sun comes up. Sometimes the name will be 'Bluish-Light-of-Dawn,' or 'Arrow-of-the-Sun,' or 'Tall-Broken-Pine.' As beautiful as the names in your Litany of the Blessed Virgin." And before the astonished priest could utter a word, the man was reciting one of the most beautiful parts of the litany with cadenced rhythm and respect. "Tower-of-Ivory," "House-of-Gold," "Ark-of-the-Covenant," "Gate-of-Heaven," "Morning-Star"; to which the padre replied with a fervent "Pray for us," after each allusion.

"How on earth do you account for the primitive's urge for metaphorical expression?" he asked the now completely bewildered young priest.

But the padre had to ask him a question before they progressed any further in the unusual conversation, and to it the man replied, "A Catholic? Heavens, no! I'm a minister's son. But I have always been interested in that litany because I believe it sprang out of the 'Courtly School of Love.' My Harvard English professor, however, did not agree.

"But, to continue with the baptism. You see, when a child is born in Isleta, a curious duty devolves upon the father. For eight days he must keep a fire going in the fireplace; no matter what the weather is, the fire must not go out, day or night. If I had let it die, there would have been only one way to rekindle it. I would have had to go to the adobe of the *cacique,* the spiritual head of the pueblo, who always has a fire, and take a light from it without attracting his attention, which is often a hard thing to do. But I was very fortunate in that my fire did not go out, and my Rainbow-of-the-Sun is well on the way to being as beautiful as her mother."

Here the little man relaxed and sighed happily; but seeing the concern in the face of the missionary, he hastened to add, "But, Father, you need not worry. With few exceptions all the Indians have their children baptized your way. Only those who are believers in the ways of old follow the custom I have just described. But,

The Padre of Isleta

heavens! I did not come here to tell you all this. I came to find out about you. The sacristan tells me you are French. Is that correct?"

There was no challenge in the eyes this time, only friendly eagerness, and as the man settled himself more comfortably on the hard chair, the priest noticed for the first time that one arm hung limp at his side. The guest must have sensed his interest, for he said simply, "Paralysis from overwork on the Los Angeles *Times*." And Father Docher in order to change the subject, reluctantly began to talk about himself.

"Yes, I am French. I was born in Le Crest, a medieval village of just a few hundred inhabitants. It is an interesting place. The old stone houses are built at different levels on the side of a crag, where a tower remains as the last remnant of a castle in ruins. Most of the buildings were destroyed in the wars frequent in the history of Auvergne, or during the French Revolution, but the beautiful church is still in existence, as well as a monastery."

Here the voice of the speaker suddenly changed. The listener looked at him sharply and realized that he was slipping thousands of miles away to the land of his heritage, hundreds of years away in time, and that he, curiously enough, was going with him; not on a tide of sentimentality, however; he couldn't as yet define the overtones of emotion in the voice of the young priest as he continued. "It was a land where the First Crusade was preached by Peter the Hermit, and where the echoes of the famous, *'Dieu lo vult'* shouted by the assembly of the first knights to volunteer will live forever in the hearts of the people."

The distant sound of a tom-tom, and the answering call of a passing youth brought the priest back to reality. "Mah-ee-kah!" interpreted the visitor casually. "Only a call for the youths to go to the *estufa*. Go on with the story, Padre. How did you happen to become a priest?"

"Becoming a priest doesn't happen," he answered. And again the unfamiliar gleam appeared in the grey eyes, as he said, "It too is a 'call.' I was eighteen years of age when I began my studies for the priesthood at St. Sauver's Seminary in Puy-de-Dome. Those eight years were hard because work in the vineyards at home necessitated irregular schooling. But life is strange," he went on. Here the caller glanced up from an old Navajo rug he had been looking at during

Father Docher's First Caller

most of the recital, as if in anticipation of something interesting. Once again, this time closer and more insistent, came the drumbeats, and the answering cry of the pueblo youths, "Mah-ee-kah," "Mah-ee-kah."

"In those days, ecclesiastical students not in Major Orders were not exempt from military duty. I was in my first year of philosophy in the Grand Seminary of Clermont-Ferrand, and twenty-seven years old, when I put on red trousers and was off to fight in the French-Colonial wars."

"Well, that must have been an interesting interlude in the life of a young scholastic," interrupted the caller. "You no doubt learned a great deal about life and men on the battlefield. Just what was the French-Colonial situation at that time? My memory needs some help."

"You remember that up to 1880 no special attempt had been made, or success achieved by any European power in establishing special advantages for herself in China, though the French had gained—"

"Now I remember," the caller again interrupted. "Because some French missionaries were murdered in an area south of China, Napoleon III sent an expedition which conquered and annexed what is known as French Cochin China in 1862. Is that right?" And without waiting for an answer, he hurried on. "The Chinese didn't have a chance. Neither had the Indian. The Anglos just moved in on them. Don't look loyal and patriotic, Father. There will be plenty of time for argument later on. Tell me, how in heaven's name did you land away out here?"

In spite of the man's seeming interest in his life's history, the padre knew that the next part must be hurried over. There were confessions to be heard at four o'clock. Besides, one could never tell this apparent ethnologist, historian, poet, what had followed: the breakdown of the soldier, the long invalidism at Le Crest, the worry and fear of his mother and sister that weak lungs would prevent the fulfillment of an ideal, the power of prayer in making possible the completion of the silvered design in the pattern of his life—these were things of which one could not speak to a stranger. Just as there were things of which one should not speak, memories one had to forget, but that somehow were always present. The beauty and fragrance of his mother's little serre, feathered pink carnations,

The Padre of Isleta

Immortelles and Muguets. The visitor followed the young missionary's gaze out of the window; he, too, saw sand and dried tumbleweed, and the withered roots of a tamarisk tree, but the eyes which met his as Father Docher continued in an impersonal manner to finish the story were merely those of an alert and confident young man.

"And so," he continued quickly, "Sergeant Docher was sent home after a year on the battlefields of Cochin-China. But I finally recovered my health after a long period of invalidism in Le Crest, finished my studies for the priesthood, and volunteered to come to New Mexico for missionary work with Father Eguillon—was ordained at Santa Fe, said my first mass in St. Francis Cathedral, missioned to Taos for a year, and here I am."

The little man in the strange garb stood up, brought his moccasined feet together, lifted the good arm in military salute, and said with a smile, " 'El Padre Sargento'. That is what you will be to us. How is this for a christening? We are going to be friends, I know."

"But you haven't even told me your name," said the priest, as he answered the salute.

"Oh, yes, I forgot that completely. Lummis, Charles Fletcher Lummis. I will come again in a few days and bring you my book, *A Tramp Across the Continent,* published not so long ago. I think you will like it. It is all about a strange 'call' that I had. Not quite as strange as the one you, or the soldier-priest who is buried in the church had—"

Father Docher leaned forward. "You mean Father Padilla, of course. Tell me about him."

"Ah! that is another story, padre. One that you can get from the Indians themselves. Now, my 'call' merely took me on a one hundred and forty day walk. To be exact, three thousand, seven hundred and five miles, or the distance from Chillicothe to Los Angeles, including detours. I didn't miss a thing on the way; in fact, I broke my arm seeing the natural wonders of the West. I set it myself, too. But I will let you read the book; it gives full details."

And with a *hasta la vista,* Charles Fletcher Lummis departed leaving the new missionary staring after him in amazement.

3

Kimo the Lion-Hearted

"KIMO the lion-hearted is dying. He wants you."

Patricio stood in the study, turning his big hat in his hands. He ran nervous fingers through his hair and stamped his feet to remove the snow. As the padre pulled on his overcoat and wrapped his muffler about his throat, Patricio talked on—"Kimo is old. He has forgotten the number of years as the white man counts them, but he is as old as a tall pine tree on Eagle Feather Mountain; one that was only so high when he was born many snows ago. Because he is old, death should be easy for him, but he turns on his pallet of rugs and is restless. He said that he could find peace only when you come to talk to him."

Father Docher pulled the door of the study behind them and stepped out into the glistening snow. Automatically he glanced at the sky where the ashy-grey clouds frayed out into blackness.

Patricio, following the direction of the priest's eyes, pointed up, circling out the horizon rim. "It is the earth bowl, turned over us. Now we can see it. Sometimes it is so when death is near."

When the two reached the home of Kimo, Father Docher went in and knelt by the dying man. He listened to him closely, for the voice was faint as a child's when sick. The Indian and the white man watched for an hour by his side after the Last Sacraments were administered, and then suddenly Patricio said softly, "He is gone. He who was a great strength, like a sheep he went. I must go to tell the Chief of the Corn Group."

The assistant to the Chief of the Corn Group went to the home of Kimo. He sprinkled meal of the yellow corn from the feet of the dead man in a straight line to the doorway. So may the dead have a pathway that their feet may not stumble. When he left, an aunt of the deceased entered. She too was old and trembling, but she

The Padre of Isleta

carefully brushed the hair of the dead man with cotton and a twig brush dipped in the water from a bowl she carried. She washed the face with water from the same bowl, threw the remaining water to the four directions, and broke the bowl on the floor, so that it would never again be used by hands of mortal man. She folded the hands of the dead man together, and on the middle fingers placed a cross of *perlin*. As the last act of the Indian ritual, she covered the body with an Indian blanket, a *manta*.

The next morning was cold and frostily clear. Father Docher led a procession through the snow from the dead man's house to the church. Four men followed him carrying the body in a blanket. Mass was said for the repose of the soul of the dead. On the day following, the priest again led the procession to the front of the church, for to the Indian three days must elapse before the body is buried. Father Docher walked before them, carrying a cross in his hands, and when the body was placed head west, facing the rising sun, he pronounced the last words the living may give for the dead, and watched them throw earth on the blanket.

After Father Docher returned to the church, the Corn Chief drew a circle with an arrow around the grave, for the dead must have protection from witches—for should a person be "witched to death," four days pass and the witches exhume the body and so get-another-child or a witch to torment the people.

The relatives of the dead man stayed in the house for four days, or four years by their ritual. On the third day all went to the river and washed their heads in yucca roots and water. The fourth day before sun up, all went again to the river and sprinkled meal on the water; then they bathed, carefully washing away contamination. They returned to the village and did not look backward, for the deceased might follow. That evening they joined in a ceremony in the death room, when the Corn Fathers arrived and made a meal altar, surrounded by arrow points and prayer feathers, with a meal path to the door—a way for the deceased to enter and gain food so that on his long journey he would not be hungry.

The Chief chanted at the doorway, "You cannot see him, but you hear footsteps and fumbling. Enter you and eat." He sprinkled another pathway for the spirit to leave. The Chief took food and prayer feathers, ran from the village, came back, closed the door,

Kimo the Lion-Hearted

and made a cross over it. So was the spirit of the dead man closed out forever.

Thus was the Indian, called Kimo, buried by the Christian rites and by the Indian rites of nature. And the words he had whispered to Father Docher, as he leaned over him at the moment of his passing, had been, "What if my spirit should be flying, clothed in the robes of the angels, and the spirits of my people in their round of eternal hunting should shoot me with an arrow, thinking me to be an eagle? It is hard for me, this dying. Harder for me than for you. You have only the one way to trouble the spirit, and I must struggle with **two.**"

4

Los Lunas

MOST of the members of the Los Lunas parish were waiting to greet Father Docher when he came out of the church after saying his first mass in that settlement. The newly arrived missionary appreciated their friendly welcome, and chatted happily with them as they walked out to the road which tied the village to history. He enjoyed meeting the Luna family, for whom the largest and prettiest settlement between Albuquerque and Belen had been named, and also Mrs. Louis Huning, of whom Mr. Lummis had told him. He was just about to accept Mrs. Luna's invitation to breakfast when Tomás, who had come with him in order to serve mass, pulled at his coat and said, "But, padre, the priests always have breakfast with the Hunings." Mrs. Huning smiled at Tomás and then diplomatically remarked, "No, not always, Father. The missionaries customarily have breakfast with us, or with the Lunas, when they say mass here. We are having German pancakes this morning, and I guess Tomás must have known."

"Well, we will look forward to having you the next time you come then," said the charming Spanish lady, as she shook hands with the priest. "Tomás, I promise to have something almost as good as the Huning pancakes."

Father Docher was grateful for such evidences of kindness, and he was also hungry, so in a few minutes he and Tomás were in the Huning parlor "making themselves at home" while their hostess went to inform the servants there would be guests for breakfast. As he sat down, he recalled Mr. Lummis' remarks concerning Mrs. Huning. "She is a very intelligent woman," he had said, "and what will undoubtedly please your soul is the fact that she has read herself into the Catholic church. She hasn't converted her husband yet, though," Lummis had added jokingly. "You know, padre," he

Los Lunas

had gone on in a confidential mood, "whenever I get to the point where I think that I have forgotten about the ways of the white man, I go to call on the Hunings. I sit in the parlor and look at the things which make for the dignity of living. I like lace curtains, beautiful carpets, and upholstered chairs. I like the hospitality of such gracious people; the efficiency with which such a home is run, and, heaven knows, I like the discipline evident in their four well-bred children."

"But," he continued, rolling a cigarette, "I see dignity of life also in the Indian adobe in which I have lived for the past five years. I have a bed, a chair, and an old table, at the present time littered with my notes of *The Land of Poco Tiempo*. I eat chili and beans, and mutton stew, day after day, as do all the members of the Abeita family from whom I rented the room. But there is peace there, too, and respect for the fundamental realities of their way of life. Queer, isn't it, padre, that my nature responds just as readily to the ordered beauty of Indian cultural patterns as it does to the cultural background obvious in the Huning household? Do you think that I am odd, padre?"

But the padre had felt that he needed time in which to think about his new friend's approach to Indian life before committing himself on what he thought were its obvious limitations for a Harvard scholar, so he said, with a chuckle, "I expected nothing so interesting as you in Isleta, Mr. Lummis." And to this remark, the scholar had quickly replied, "Well, I must admit that I have met more interesting men than you, padre. You are too much of a conformist for me. But, for some reason, I like you. I guess it is your sense of humor, or the fact that you haven't tried to convert me."

Father Docher smiled now, as he caught a reflection of himself in a great gold-framed mirror which hung above the fireplace in the Huning home. He hadn't sat in an upholstered chair since leaving France, and he was obviously enjoying himself. So, too, was the Indian boy, surreptitiously touching the keys of the great square piano, his eyes following in childish awe tiny prisms of sunbeams reflected on the keyboard by a cut-glass candelabrum nearby.

It would be a hard thing to say whether the priest or the acolyte enjoyed the breakfast the more. The pancakes which Tomás ate were not counted, neither were the cups of coffee which the padre

The Padre of Isleta

drank. As they ate, Mrs. Huning talked of many things. She told of her home in Bremen, of coming to Los Lunas as a bride, of her conversion to Catholicism, and of her and her husband's plans for the education of their children in St. Louis. She also told of the castle which her husband's brother, Franz Huning, had built in Albuquerque, to the amazement of everyone in the little town.

"And why a castle in the wilderness? Has it a drawbridge?" inquired the padre.

"No, but a moat," laughingly responded his hostess, "the Rio Grande. The beautiful castle is the fulfillment of a boyish dream. It is the exact duplicate of one on the Rhine that my brother-in-law loved. My husband will probably make a trip to Albuquerque for supplies for the store when he returns from the sheep ranches. Perhaps, if your duties permit, you could go with him, and have a visit with the Franz Hunings." But the padre shook his head over the proposed all-day trip, and Tomás looked sad.

"Well, some other time," continued Mrs. Huning, "if not this spring, Father. And Tomás, if you are a good boy, you can go sometime, too, when we are taking the children."

And Tomás, who had always longed to ride far, far to the east where the Sandias held up the sky, or far, far to the west where the volcanoes pointed skyward, knew that Albuquerque lay somewhere in between these far places. It would be a long, long ride, and he hung his head in order to hide his happiness.

"What is Mr. Lummis doing these days? I haven't seen him lately," Mrs. Huning asked, as she led the way back to the parlor to get the newspapers she always saved for the missionaries.

"So many things I can't keep track of him. Every time I see him he has a new job on hand. A ruin to measure, a book to finish, a folk-tale to write, a wild pony to break, or a footrace to run with an Indian boy. Just at present he is very much excited over a new kodak he has."

"A new black box," said Mrs. Huning. "You should have been here when he first appeared with his kodak hanging across his shoulder. A 'hechercero', the Indians would say to me. They were sure that he had been bewitched, and that the 'little black box' had something to do with his paralyzed arm. He has taken thousands of

View of Padre Docher's residence at Isleta.

Los Lunas

pictures, I imagine, since coming, but he certainly got into serious trouble one time over 'the kodak business'."

The padre looked up from a month-old paper she had given him to scan. She didn't have to ask him if he wanted to hear the story, but continued:

"One of his best friends around here is Don Manuel Antonio Chavez, whose *hacienda* is at San Mateo, forty-five miles this side of Acoma. All the members of the Chavez family like Mr. Lummis because he converses at great length in fluent Spanish about his hobbies, and his poems, and his books. He loves to sing Spanish songs, too, so he is always a welcome visitor. Well, one Holy Week he went over to San Mateo especially to see the Penitentes. Because he was such a good friend of Don Manuel's, he was allowed to watch some of the rites, but when he got out 'the little black box' and began to take pictures, that was a different story. They threw rocks at him, but he went right ahead and took a picture of the Cristo on the Cross."

The padre's eyebrows shot up, and his eyes bulged. He knew that the medieval penitential practice of self-flagellation still existed in remote New Mexico villages, in spite of the fact that the Church had condemned such fanatical practices. But in spite of prayers, pleas, and threats of excommunication on the part of the clergy, the unearthly wail of a reed whistle in some mountain-bounded fastness each Good Friday meant that the secret ceremonies, often reaching almost actual crucifixion, were being held. In exact proportion to the serious objection of the Church to such a cult, was the objection of its members to even observation of their secret rites by the curious, and "only fools," so the padre had heard, dared to make their presence known.

"And so?" he urged.

"And so," repeated Mrs. Huning, with a dramatic shrug of her shoulders, "the Penitentes had a secret meeting, according to Don Manuel's son Ireneo, and appointed a committee of three members to punish Mr. Lummis. In order to escape, Ireneo drove him twenty-five miles from the ranch to the railway station at Grants, where he took the train for Isleta. But the Penitente committee went across the country by horseback, boarded the same train at Laguna, followed Mr. Lummis home, and late that night they fired a charge of

The Padre of Isleta

buckshot through the window at him as he got up from the table where he had been writing. One shot lodged in his neck, and was almost the end of him.

"When the news reached San Mateo, Amado Chavez went to Isleta and took Mr. Lummis back to San Mateo with him. Mrs. Lummis came from California and nursed him back to health. We all thought that he would have the men who tried to kill him arrested, but he didn't do a thing about it, other than explain to them about 'the kodak business', and strange as it may seem they all became good friends. But the man learned a lesson."

"What a story," said the priest, exhaling his breath in a little whistle. "I suppose it is just one of many you know. I am beginning to realize that there is every variety and kind in this new land of my adoption."

"You haven't met Adolphe Bandelier yet, have you Father?" inquired Mrs. Huning. "He is the one who can tell you the tales. Any kind you want to hear, historical, legendary or mythological, and you may be sure that he won't scramble the facts and legends in with the myths."

"He is just the man I'm looking for," said Father Docher with a conclusive head shake.

"I know," smiled Mrs. Huning, "the Padilla legend is disturbing your days and nights."

"Exactly. I will have to ask my countryman about that."

"Oh, but he isn't French, Father. He was born in Switzerland, although his people have lived in Highland, Illinois, for many years. If you ever meet a big man hiking along the road carrying a stick, pockets bulging with papers, you will know at once that he is Mr. Bandelier. He walks from village to village, or from ruin to ruin, spending months at a time in some isolated place in order to get all the ethnological or archæological facts possible. He often stops to see us, so covered with dirt and dust that he won't come into the house until he has had a thorough scrubbing in the barn. He says he doesn't mind or fear anything but 'piojos' however."

"Are they one of those wild tribes in Arizona?" the new missionary ventured.

Mrs. Huning had given Tomás a bag of cookies to take home, but he had promptly eaten them, and at this point in the conversation

Los Lunas

was under a chair in a highly successful hunt for crumbs. On hearing the padre's remark he snickered audibly and began to crawl out on all fours.

"Not only in Arizona, but we have thousands of them in New Mexico. You will have to be very careful Father," cautioned Mrs. Huning with great seriousness. "They steal upon the enemy unawares and torture him, not to death, of course, but a prolonged attack would certainly cause one to lose his mind. Ask Tomás about them. It is only recently that he has escaped from their clutches."

"*Mon Dieu*," exclaimed the priest, looking in consternation at the little server. "Tomás, why haven't you told me of this?"

But Tomás was apparently very busy wiping his mouth on his sleeve, and Mrs. Huning, seeing that the little joke had gone far enough, laughed merrily, as her bright blue eyes met the child's black ones in fun-loving acknowledgment of his contribution to its success.

"Only head lice, Father. I must give you some of my soap to take home. Although the clergy seem to escape the common pestilence, it may come in handy some day."

Father Docher laughed as he hadn't done in months, and he suddenly felt that he had been a long time without such an outlet for the body and the soul. As he got up to leave, Mrs. Huning picked up a few books for him to take back to read. "You will especially enjoy Mr. Bandelier's *The Delight Makers*," she said. "When I read the manuscript I told him that it would not only make him famous, but rich. He couldn't get an American publisher interested in it at first. In Germany, however, they recognized his genius and published the first edition of the story.

"I must tell you, before you go, about the beautiful manuscript he began to prepare at the suggestion of Archbishop Salpointe. A fourteen hundred page history of the colonization of New Mexico, Arizona, and Sonora and Chihuahua, Mexico. He wrote it in French, and illustrated it with about four hundred watercolor sketches. Archbishop Chapelle was so pleased with it that he sent it to Pope Leo XIII for his Golden Jubilee, and the Holy Father was so appreciative of its value that he put it in the Vatican Library. I am telling you these things, Father, because he won't. He is the most modest scholar you will ever meet; you will enjoy him, I know."

The Padre of Isleta

Tomás climbed into the buggy, holding another bag of cookies, the home-made soap, and a leg of lamb. Father Docher carried the books, the St. Louis newspapers, and some geranium slips. Each also carried home with him another gift, as did all of Mrs. Huning's friends, a golden strand, out of which the years wove a tapestry of beautiful memories.

5

The Legend of Father Padilla

"WHAT is it that worries the people of Isleta?" Father Docher asked Emeliano one night. The caretaker of the church and *Convento* piled the cedar logs by the fireplace in the study. He carefully straightened each log and sat back as if studying the effect of wood piled high against adobe wall.

For the past two weeks the priest had been aware of a certain tenseness among the Indians. At times he had come upon men gathered into tight groups and at his approach they had separated and drifted away. The women, drawn into their shawls, hurried swiftly about the village and kept the children close about them. Vague, remote, it was a nameless fear that Father Docher felt in the Isleta people. Tonight he asked the question casually, hardly expecting an answer.

Suddenly Emeliano straightened and looked directly at the priest. But the priest, having learned a great deal about Indians during his past year, stared only at the fire leaping high in the chimney, and he seemed to be listening only to the wind—a flute with a thin high wailing in the winter night.

"Tashide," and as Father Docher glanced up at the unaccustomed title, Emeliano permitted a smile of pleased recognition at the priest's notice. "Tashide," he repeated again. "That is what we are calling you now, for you are friendly to us. It is an Indian word—it means, how shall I say it? It means, 'Little Priest,' or 'Little Helper.' We call only those whom we respect, 'Little Helper'."

Father Docher relaxed and sank back in his chair. He lighted his pipe again with a twist of corn-husk touched from the glowing fire. The first recognition that he had had in spoken words of his work in the pueblo.

Emeliano talked on in a half monotone. "Well, you ask me what

The Padre of Isleta

is the matter here in Isleta. We are afraid. You see, Father Padilla is stirring again in his coffin and strange things are happening in the village."

"Father Padilla, the priest buried in the church by the altar? I have heard something about him, but—" the priest spoke softly, as if afraid to break the spell of the teller's mood.

Emeliano hesitated again, and then he said, "That priest, he has been buried a long time there, but he moves, and then strange things—"

"What things, Emeliano?"

"Well, there are noises. When I close the church at night, I hear them up by the altar. And when I open it early in the morning I hear a thumping. Twice I have seen a strange figure by the corral in back of the church, and Maria has heard strange noises in the square in front of the church where our dead are buried."

Again he shifted and stared long at the fire. "The night you came, it was dark you remember? Maria thought at first you were Father Padilla when you knocked at the door because you were strange and wore a long black overcoat. But his body was not moving then. Now, the coffin has been rising."

Father Docher turned slightly in his chair. "Father Padilla, the Franciscan friar who came with Coronado's band. The white man's history says that the missionary priest, Father Padilla, has been dead about four hundred years and that no one knows where he is buried." Again, a silence as Emeliano said nothing. So the priest continued, "The history of the white man also says there was no church in Isleta in 1542."

Emeliano twisted a corn-husk absently. "My father said there was a church then. His father told him so." He shook his head sadly. "You do not understand, Tashide. It is because you are a white man, and because you are new and strange here too. I think it will be all right if I tell you about it.

"In the early days the parish stretched to Laguna and to Acoma. Then the priest traveled from Isleta for mass in each village. Much as you do now, Tashide, going from here to the villages of Los Lunas and Peralta and Los Padillas. Then, too, he was called for confession and for rites for the dying. Once an Indian at Laguna lay dying. A messenger came to tell the Father to hurry. So Father Padilla rode

The Legend of Father Padilla

through the day. He reached the pueblo before the death of the Indian, and administered the rites of the church for those who go to seek the Great Father. After the man was at peace, Father Padilla started the long trip back to Isleta. It was dusk and the snow was falling. He rode into the night and lost his way. After a long time he saw a light, and he stopped at the house, but he did not know the woman who answered. She gave him the way, and then asked him in for a cup of coffee, when he told her who he was. But as he was drinking the coffee, there was a loud pounding at the door, and heavy curses. It was the woman's husband. He had come home drunk and mad. He was a Mexican gambler and had lost money at cards. It was very bad. He yelled at the woman, called her a fat dog, and then stabbed the Father as he sat at the table. Then the woman screamed, 'El Padre, El Padre.' When the man saw what he had done, he got sorry. He picked the body up, and carried it out to the yard, and put it on the horse. He tied each boot to a stirrup, and the hands to the pommel of the saddle. Then he roped the stirrups together under the horse's belly, and headed the horse into the blackness.

"Early the next morning an Isleta woman went to the well for water and she saw the horse standing at the gate of the churchyard with the body slumped over the pommel of the saddle. She ran for her husband."

Emeliano sat quietly. "After such a death, how could the poor priest rest? The Indians buried him near the altar where one so holy should rest. But he doesn't rest. His body rises in the coffin, and pushes up the dirt in the floor. We put down boards, but now the boards rise. We think he is walking in the village at night."

Father Docher leaned over the hearth and knocked his pipe on the adobe. How historical facts had been twisted into legends to fit the needs of the people. The only Spanish settlement in 1540 had been that of Coronado's group that wintered at Tiguex—now Bernalillo —so, historically speaking, there could have been no Mexican gambler—no church to bury him in—no—but Emiliano sensing the doubt in the priest's mind hastened on, "All of our ancestors know about Father Padilla, and that he lived here. I will show you where the coffin is pushing up."

Father Docher picked up a candle, and led the way through the

The Padre of Isleta

sacristy into the sanctuary. Emeliano hesitated a moment, crossed himself, and then pointed to a board under the gospel side of the main altar. At a nod from the priest he lifted it up. The hard earth was cracked, and as they looked one of the cracks deepened.

Emeliano dropped the board suddenly, crossed himself quickly, and hurried from the church, leaving the priest to follow.

Back in the study Emeliano frowned in worry. "Sometime, somebody must help the soul of the friar. He must not wander forever. I go now. We don't like to be out in the night when he walks the streets of the village, for if we see him we suffer sickness or even death." And Father Docher was left to ponder the fear of the Indians and the fate of the Franciscan father.

Charles Fletcher Lummis, ready to mount his pony at Isleta. Lummis and Padre Docher were close friends in the early nineties.

6

Adolphe Bandelier Visits the Padre

"WHAT on earth are you excavating an *acequia* for, Father? That is no place to look for evidences of prehistoric man."

The padre laughed as he stopped digging, and turned to look at the speaker. He saw a big, friendly, dust stained traveler. "You must be Adolphe Bandelier, about whom I have heard so much," exclaimed the Father as he extended his hand. "I had begun to think that you had passed through to the Hopiland without stopping for a visit."

"Never that, Father, I have too many friends here. Has my friend Charles Lummis interested you in archæology? That is one of his missions in life," he went on as he put down the walking stick and sat on the bank of the big ditch.

"No, he thinks I am a hopeless student and doesn't bother much about what my contribution will be in that field. I was just getting a few buckets of this good dirt. I have found that by mixing it with goat manure it makes an excellent fertilizer. Horse manure burns the young plants. Of course, I strain it several times. But, Mon Dieu, why should I stand here in the presence of a great scholar and speak of manure!"

"Every bit as important," said the scientist with an appreciative and evaluating glance at the short, stocky figure in a badly fitting black suit, and celluloid Roman collar.

"Come, then. You will see the beginning of what I hope will some day be a garden. We will stop and get Mr. Lummis. He has just returned from the Enchanted Mesa. Got some wonderful pictures this time. I will have a special dish for our supper."

Mr. Bandelier smiled as he picked up the stick and one of the buckets of reddish-looking mud. "I know what you are having today, and every day. Frijoles and mutton stew, and the mutton you dried on the clothes line. Any flies in Isleta, Father? I'm really

The Padre of Isleta

disappointed ... Here, I thought you would have some nice greens for me."

"I am truly sorry," apologized the missionary. "The ground is so hard and the seeds so scarce. Some day, though—"

"I was only teasing. I have been thankful for the scraps thrown to the dogs. Such has often been the case, until I won the friendship of the particular tribe I was studying. It was that, or starve to death, Father. Now, in my opinion there is nothing better than beans cooked in an Indian pot, for hours and hours."

"With a little onion," added the priest, as he picked up the other bucket and swung along by the side of the great archæologist.

Later that evening, after the three men had finished the supper of frijoles and mutton stew, they sat on the long porch of the *Convento* and talked of many things before the padre led up to the subject of Father Padilla. Charles Lummis threw up his hands when Father Docher finished telling Emeliano's version of the legend. "There," he exclaimed, "you have a perfect example of what causes a historian to lose his mind. It is my theory that our Indian friend has dragged poor Father Latrado into the tale, the priest whom the Indians murdered in this vicinity in 1630. I found an inscription on Inscription Rock not long ago, made by one Lujan 'who passed that way' on March 23, 1632, to avenge the death of Latrado. What do you think, Adolphe?"

"It is possible," responded Mr. Bandelier. "I have never heard any version similar to the one Father has just told us. The one generally believed in Isleta, in regard to Padilla, is that the men of the village were sent to bring back the body from the land of the Quivira. There is also another legend to the effect that by some mysterious means the body of the murdered priest was transported to the church here. I have been making a few notes, and doing some research on the man. The story interests me."

Here Adolphe Bandelier arose from his chair and began to walk back and forth on the portal, the eyes of both listeners following the big figure.

"Castañeda mentions him of course, so does Torquemada. Mota Padilla gives a more comprehensive account, however. It is known that Father Padilla was a native of Andalusia, Spain, and comparatively young and vigorous when he obtained permission from his Provincial in Mexico to join Coronado's band. It would appear from the records left by the ones mentioned, that Father Padilla was as strict as he was zealous, and watched over the conduct of the men carefully. It is possible that he accompanied Coronado to the Staked Plains, after 'the Turk' had convinced the great Conqueror that there was fabulous wealth to be found there, but that is not so important to us as the fact that he remained in New Mexico after Coronado broke camp at Tiguex in 1542 and left for Mexico. If Padilla ever did come to Isleta for missionary work, which the Indians believe that he did, then he must have come between that time and the time we know he left for missionary work in the Quivira country, which has been quite definitely proven was in the fall of 1542. Do you agree, Mr. Lummis?"

"I am not enough of an authority on that period of New Mexico history to say. Sounds all right to me, Adolphe. Go on with the story. But why in heavens name don't you sit down? Haven't you had enough hiking today? You make me nervous."

"Apparently, Father Padilla was kindly treated by the tribe of Indians he found there, but he decided to leave and carry the word of God to another tribe farther on," Mr. Bandelier continued, without any recognition of his good friend's remarks. "And that is just where he made a mistake, Father. A missionary who has been well treated by one tribe cannot leave that tribe without exposing himself to the danger of being looked upon as a traitor by the friends made. You see, Padilla exposed himself to the double danger of being looked upon by his first acquaintances as a traitor who abandoned them in order to impart to others the benefits of his wisdom; and, by those to whom he went, as an enemy coming from people with whom they were at war.

"Castañeda says that the friar intended to go to the Guyas, a tribe with whom the Quiviras were at war, and that the latter therefore killed him. Jaramillo gives no such an account. He attributed his death to the cupidity of the Quiviras, and states that Indians from Tiguex had instructed them to perform the deed.

"According to Mota Padilla, the friar left Quivira with a small escort, against the will of the Indians of that village, who loved him as a father. But at the end of one day's journey, he was met by

The Padre of Isleta

Indians on the warpath, and fearing their evil intentions he requested the Portuguese, who, you remember, Mr. Lummis, also remained in Tiguex after the departure of the Spaniards, to flee—"

"I didn't remember," said Lummis, "but continue. It is really very interesting."

"Yes, a soldier named Andreas Docampo, as well as two boys named Lucus and Sebastian, fled upon the Franciscan's request that they do so, and the blessed Father, kneeling down, offered up his life, which he sacrificed for the good of the souls of the others. To quote Mota Padilla, 'He thus realized his most ardent desire, the felicity of martyrdom by the arrows of those barbarians, who afterwards threw his body into a pit and covered it with innumerable rocks.' The Portuguese and the two boys, upon returning to Quivira, gave notice of what had happened and the natives felt it deeply on account of the love they had for Father Padilla. Don Pedro de Tober, in some papers which he wrote and left at the town of Culiacan, states that the Indians killed the blessed Father in order to obtain his ornaments, and that there was a tradition of miraculous signs connected with his death, such as comets and balls of fire. That is all I know, Father, about the legend of Father Padilla, and the life of Father Padilla," said the great scholar quietly and modestly, as he stopped pacing and sat down.

"You should write what you have just told us," suggested Father Docher, "so that others may benefit also. It has been a privilege to listen to the results of your research. I have already decided what I will do in regard to the situation here in Isleta concerning the first Christian martyr in New Spain. I have been considerably worried."

"I may follow your suggeston and write an article," replied Adolphe Bandelier. "In fact I may do it before I go to bed. I think—"

"Tell me," interrupted Charles Lummis, "do you always do a marathon when in the throes of organizing material? I am exhausted from just watching you."

"Always. Didn't you know that? Just one of my idiosyncracies," retorted Mr. Bandelier with a twinkle in his eyes as he looked at the Indian rings on Charles Lummis' hands, the moccasins on his feet and the bright belt around his waist. "Practically every bit of my *Final Report* for the Archeological Society of America was

Adolphe Bandelier Visits the Padre

organized in just such a manner. I pace up and down and then I write, and then I pace up and down and then I write."

"Lord, man, that's awful," groaned Lummis. "I'm calling off the joint expedition to Peru, Father; how can I live with such energy. And I'll bet he has hiked twenty miles today, in addition to the display we have just witnessed."

"Only thirteen miles," laughed Mr. Bandelier. "I left Albuquerque this morning. But I have to make better time tomorrow. I think I will take the bed, and you can sleep on the floor tonight, Charles."

"I shall be honored to sleep at your feet," bantered the other scholar. "I have already fixed the bed for my distinguished guest."

"What time do you say Mass, Father?" asked Mr. Bandelier, as he turned to say goodnight at the gate, where Father Docher had walked with his guests.

"Six o'clock," came the answer.

"I will be there," replied Adolphe Bandelier. "We will both pray that our friend here will not fall off a cliff and break his leg before we get started for South America. I have lots of work mapped out for him to do."

7

An Ethnologist's Viewpoint

EARLY the next morning Father Docher walked with Bandelier as he started westward to Hopiland. As they passed through the patio the drums for a dance for planting sounded, muffled. Father Docher kept his eyes on the ground as he listened to the throbbing beats.

"*Buenas dias,* Emeliano." It was Bandelier greeting the caretaker. "Are you joining the men in the kiva so early in the morning?"

Emeliano shook his head. "No, I am going over to the store for flour. Always the women need something in their cooking, when a store is not far away."

Father Docher looked at Emeliano, his mind still occupied with the drum-beats. "Emeliano, what do you think of this dance for planting?"

Emeliano glanced from the corner of his eye at the priest. There were some things a white man could never understand. Well, this priest had been in the pueblo a year and he was friendly. Bandelier, of course, was accepted.

"I will tell you a story, Father. There was a happening, as the Indians tell it, that would interest you. Once there was a struggle between the Catholic God, *Kika'awei* Dius, and the Indian God, *Kika'awei* Waeide. They wanted to claim the souls of the Indians, each in his own way. To show his power, they decided to see who could throw the stronger. Our Father Waeide said, 'Well, Elder Brother, you throw to that spruce tree.' Our Father Dius shot with his gun to the spruce tree and the bullet went through it. Father Waeide shot with his bow and arrow. With his power he made lightning which struck the tree and shattered it. 'Well, younger brother, you are more powerful than I. You have beaten me,' said Elder Brother. 'Let us try another way and see who will have the people.' So Father Dius, with his power, built a church and rang

An Ethnologist's Viewpoint

the bells and the people came and came and came. While the priest was saying Mass at the altar, Waeide came with his drum and standing in front of the church began to beat. All of the people went out leaving the priest alone. For Waeide had more power and Elder Brother answered, 'You have more power and you have beaten me'."

Emeliano had stopped suddenly and leaned over and flecked an imaginary spot of dust from his moccasin. Then he shook his head. "I should not have told you this, for every one knows a bear or a wild animal will get me and hurt me. That always happens if we tell our legends or rituals."

He looked relieved as he saw the store. Here was something real, something a man could understand.

"Adios, my friends. I think I will buy candy too for the children; or maybe cookies." His voice was lost in the interior of the adobe building as he left behind the strange things white men were curious about.

Bandelier strode along. "Now," he was saying, "there is still the question to be solved as to where this village was first located. Lummis thinks it has never changed since it was founded, but I can't agree with that."

Father Docher's eyes twinkled. "A walk with you is an education within itself. To learn, I must listen, and I'm afraid I was considering the story our friend Emeliano just told us."

They had reached the refuse heap west of the town and Bandelier stopped and scraped carefully with a stick. "Well, take the story Emeliano just told us about the struggle between the Catholic God, Dius, and the Indian God, Waeide—." He stopped and picked up a bit of pottery and examined it carefully, then shook his head.

"There is no doubt about it. The Indian sense of design is deteriorating, but, as I was saying—"

Father Docher stared intently at the refuse heap. To his orderly French mind there was still a sense of outrage at the Indian custom of tossing all refuse into the four heaps on the four sides of the village. But Bandelier had explained how archeologists were able to trace the development of the Indian culture by digging into these very mounds where generation after generation of Indians had thrown their refuse—bones of animals, broken pottery, and even their dead. For, only with the coming of the priests, had they been taught to bury their dead in holy ground. In times past, some of the bodies had been placed in these heaps, knees to chest, as they were in the wombs of their mothers before birth.

They walked on in silence and Father Docher began to think Bandelier had forgotten the subject of religion. Behind them the drumming sounded fainter. Bandelier watched a red-winged blackbird sweep in crimson-touched beauty to the swelling greyness of a cottonwood limb.

"Our religion for the Indians, now, Father, you will learn, is something like those cottonwood trees in spring. They are bare, but even now they are swelling full with awakening, the buds turning from the faint flush of grey to the eternal green of life. Emeliano's story states the problem of the missionary—you, to be explicit."

They climbed the softly rolling hills to the mesa land above. Bandelier walked strongly. As he talked he studied the land carefully. Always there was the possibility of finding something that told of the early life of these people.

"The pueblo Indians voluntarily accepted the new faith brought by the priests, and to a certain extent honestly. They adopted it, however, from their own peculiar standpoint; that is, they expected material benefits from it . . .

"In short, the Pueblos looked upon Christianity as upon another kind of magic, superior to the one which they practiced themselves, and they expected from the new creed greater protection from their enemies, more abundant crops, less wind, and more rain than their own magic procured. To disabuse them is extremely difficult, and yet it is being done, done through teaching, and also by the force of circumstances."

A prairie dog sat up with forepaws dangling, and then dived down into the hole. Bandelier, happy again in walking and talking, marshaled his ideas on the subject into order.

"Still, almost three hundred years of patient toil has borne some fruit; a change has crept over the religious beliefs of the Indians that renders it very difficult for the ethnologist to separate the primitive doctrine from the Christian."

The men walked on in silence, seeing the first green haze of the early spring that covered the brown mesa land. The sun beat more strongly on their backs, and Father Docher took off his hat and

Scene in front of Isleta church when friends from nearby villages of Peralta and Los Lunas are made welcome by the Indians.

An Ethnologist's Viewpoint

wiped the sweat from his forehead. Bandelier smiled at the gesture.

"Now, Father, those earlier missionaries walked from pueblo to pueblo—You will find your physical resistance increasing as the years go by. But now you had better start back to the pueblo before the sun's rays are really hot."

The priest shook his head as he deplored his inability to walk for long stretches. Bandelier rested his walking stick on the ground. "One more observation, Father, in this lecture on religion to you, a man of the cloth. There are five truths left by the missionaries who have preceded you: The idea of one Supreme Being, intercession by the saints, baptism, mass, and burial in consecrated ground. The pueblo Indians are honest in their belief of Christianity and they are equally honest in their practice of nature religion."

Father Docher wiped his forehead again. "Sometime, Mr. Bandelier, I hope you will write these observations of yours, just as you recorded those others last night."

"Sometime, Father, sometime. That word 'sometime.' Sometime I will write more of the Indian and his way of living and believing. But who will read it? I will clothe my facts in story and romance, for only when truths are so gilded will people notice. *Au revoir,* Father."

And the ethnologist turned back to the west, as the missionary advanced into a solitude so fraught with exciting facts that there never was borne to him a whisper of desolation.

8

The Church and Legend

THAT the enigma of Friar Padilla might be solved, as nearly as mortal man could solve it, and that the threads of historical facts might be untangled from the threads of legend, Father Docher talked with Archbishop Chapelle, asking and securing the cooperation of the Church in the case. The Archbishop ordered a court of inquiry to assemble all the known facts. There was no way to probe back into the past through the wavering mists of time and establish, historically, the identity of the person around whom the mystery had developed. As the Archbishop explained, the only thing the court could do was to assemble once and for all time the facts and testimonies of those who had actually had experiences in regard to the body. And so, in the spring of the year 1895, the people of Isleta, curious and yet fearing the disturbance of "him-who-had-gone-before," were massed about the outside of the church, waiting. For, on this day, the court was to be held and the body exhumed.

As a result of the investigation, the following findings were transcribed for the Archbishop, and remain to this day the only authentic document concerning the priest buried in the cottonwood coffin.

"On the 25th day of April, 1895, at 9 A. M., there met at the rectory of the Parish of San Agustín at Isleta, New Mexico, the reverend priest appointed by His Highness, the Bishop of Santa Fe, New Mexico, Most Reverend Placido Luis Chapelle, as a special committee to disinter and to examine, under the close direction of the very capable Doctor William Ruben Tipton, the supposed remains of Reverend Francisco Padilla, who had been killed by the Indians of Quivira, according to tradition three hundred fifty years before.

The Church and Legend

"This trust was undertaken by the following venerable and reverend fathers:

    Jose Maria Coudert of Bernalillo.
    James Henrique Defouri of Las Vegas.
    Luiz Maria Gentile S. J. of Albuquerque
    Juan Benito Brun of Socorro.
    Francisco Gatignol of Belen.
    Manuel Rivera of Tiptonville.
    Anton Docher of Isleta.
    Enrique Nerol (Substitute priest of Bernalillo).

"The Reverend J. M. Coudert acted as chairman in the proceedings of this investigation, and immediately after the installation of the committee, they proceeded to elect and to vote for the necessary officials in the case.

"In order to save time it was unanimously decided to name the officials by acclamation. These nominations fell on the following reverend gentlemen respectively:

    Promotor: Rev. James H. Defouri.
    Lawyer (against): Rev. J. B. Brun
    Secretary: Rev. Luiz M. Gentile S. J.
    Notary Public: Rev. M. A. Rivera.

"The following laymen were admitted as necessary assistants:

    Jose Rodriguez, native of the village and sexton of the parish.
    Benito Garcia, carpenter.
    Rafael Chavez,
    Ramon Carillo, grave diggers.

"Before our eyes the boards of the floor were lifted and the supposed body of the deceased Fray Juan Francisco Padilla was found in the very site where by local tradition he was known to have been buried.

The Padre of Isleta

"He was above the earth inside of a trough or canoe made from a cottonwood, covered by a single lid made from the same material and touching the board of the floor. The dimensions of said coffin are the following:

> Length: 6 feet and 7 inches
> Width: 17 inches
> Depth: 16 inches.

"Following are the measurements of the cadaver:

> Length: 5 feet.
> Length of the only foot found:
> 7 inches.
> Measurement of its hands:
> 7 inches.

"The body was found in a mummified state, and over his neck a stole, seemingly of purple color, and in a well preserved condition.

"The physician, Dr. W. R. Tipton, wrote a scientific report respectively of the state and condition in which the said body was found.

"Diego Abeyta whose age appears to be 90 years, and who according to his own words was sexton of the parish of San Agustín for sixty-four years, says that just prior to the time that the Indians persecuted the Spaniards (priests) and during the time that the Rev. Sanchez was priest of the place while he was still a youth, the body of the priest, Fray J. F. Padilla, came out of the earth for the first time, that it was watched for a whole night before being buried anew. The Reverend Fathers Pinon, Correa, Caballero, Valle, and Sanchez, watched and buried him. He was buried in the usual depth in the place above mentioned where we had found the body, that is near the altar to the side of the gospel. He says that the cadaver was complete at that time. He heard say that the body had in one hand a book from which one of the already mentioned priests read before the altar while shedding copious tears. At this time the sexton of the church was a man named Andrés, native of this village.

"Juan Andrés Zuni also of the same village of whose age according to him, was sixty years, declares that when for the second time the body of the priest J. F. Padilla came out above the surface of the earth, he must have been 20 years old. 'The body was,' said Andrés Zuni, 'whole, complete and dry, in a mummified state, holding a book

The Church and Legend

in his hands'; that again they buried him, but that he could not tell whether more or less deep than the first time.

"José Chiwiwi also a native and close to fifty years of age more or less declared that in his youth he had heard say that the body had arisen above the earth, and that he had seen it whole, complete and dry; that the sepulcher in which he was buried anew, was of the usual depth which covers a man of average stature. Not long after this the floor was built.

"Marcelina Lucero de Abeyta, also an Indian of the same village, fifty years old more or less, declares that while she was still a child, the body of the priest rose above the earth.

"Here end the testimonies of the first and second appearances of the body of the priest, J. F. Padilla above the surface of the earth.

"Following is what refers to a strange noise which was heard at the church the night of the 24th of December of 1889, when Reverend Andrés Eschalier was parish priest.

"Maria Marcelina Lucero says that this noise was as of someone kicking on the floor; that the altar moved and that the Indians terrified, went out of the church precipitately.

"Pablo Abeyta, Indian of the same village and about twenty-nine years, declared that the noise was audible during and while the Indians danced in the body of the church, and that the altar moved visibly.

" 'I was,' says Pablo, 'at the door of the railing (of the altar) to prevent the Indians from going in to desecrate the sanctuary.' He says that several of those present went with him to see if someone was moving the altar, but that they had not found anyone. That the dance began at 8 P. M., more or less, and that it had taken place against the authorities and without the consent of the Parish Priest.

"Having taken these testimonies with the utmost care that was possible, the body was buried anew in the same coffin. It was placed in the same place where it had lain, and in a depth of one foot. On digging this tomb, there were found human bones, a small rosary, and a bonnet (cap used by the clergy). In the coffin was placed a steel box containing a piece of paper in which is written a summary of this investigation and signed by each and everyone of those who formed this committee. "The investigation came to a close on the same day, the 25th, at noon."

9

A Christening

FATHER DOCHER walked through his orchard. It lay to the back of the church and *Convento,* sweeping down to the north fields of the Indians. The softness and gentleness of early May, after the lull of April, minimized the stark nakedness of the events of life which the winds of February and March seemed to reveal.

The trees—the pears, the apples and the plums—shivered in the breeze, releasing the light sweetness of fruit blossoms in the spring. For, as Time had spun out the life of the priest in the Indian village, the beauty growing from the soil, both in the flowers in the patio and the trees in the orchard, typified the beauty of his own France.

It was tilling time and the people of Isleta were turning the damp earth about the small growing plants. On the north barbed *cerco* a meadow-lark, cocking his head, watched the Indians in the fields beyond, and then swayed on the rail with his song. Over in the corner of the field by the orchard two men were talking. Father Docher raised his hand in greeting.

Ramon, with thumbs stuck in his belt, rocked from his toes to his heels with importance. "Last night a daughter was born to me. I am very proud, for I have three sons. Straight and strong they are, but they need a sister."

They watched the workers in the field. Joe returned to the planting, but Ramon, as is befitting a new father, was resting from the day's labors. Since the Indian line of descent is passed through the mother, pueblo men at marriage frequently go from their own clans to those of their wives. So, the birth of a daughter is a cause for celebration.

"We must name her fittingly," continued Ramon. "You will christen her in the church at the font with holy water. A Spanish name as

A Christening

is usual, but, too, I want you to give her the Indian name, in the name of the Father."

Father Docher thought of the names bestowed by the Indians, and smiled as he remembered how his tongue still twisted and stumbled when he tried to say them. He knew that eventually he would speak the Indian language, but the gutterals and inflections were hard for him with his basic knowledge of French. Time would chasten his fumbling tongue, and he would understand their words as well as their customs. Those three shots he had heard last night were Ramon's announcement to the village that a girl child had been born. Five shots would have announced a son. But Ramon was still talking.

"She will be a generous woman, for her mother was always generous when she carried the baby in her belly. She never turned her back on the fire or the sun, but faced them boldly and bravely. And I, I hunted only once in the period; then only because there was no meat. But for that hunting, the child was born gasping. Last night I ran from the village, as if chasing the deer, and then I returned quickly and passed my hands over the child—and so released the gasping."

Ramon's request for the christening was a distinct indication of the trust the people were placing in Tashide. Often they did not appear for baptism for the children and frequently, when they did, they were so encased in an air of reserve and judgment, that the act of baptism seemed to signify nothing.

But Ramon was still talking: "When the sun came over the mountain this morning, my sister carried the baby to the doorway and sprinkled the meal ground from the corn to the sun, and asked for long life for the baby. When she lifted her eyes, she saw a prayer-feather, bright and trembling. So, we shall name the baby Shiepuyu Prayer-Feather-Bright. Yes, she will be lucky."

That custom of naming the child after the first object viewed in the morning after the birth—where had he heard of it? Lummis! Of course, Lummis had told him of the naming of his own daughter that first morning he had visited him. The meadow-lark, in a final burst of song, lifted his wings and rose high in the sky and then disappeared toward the river.

On the morning of the fourth day, the baby girl was christened in

The Padre of Isleta

the rites of the Indian belief. The front room was lined with relatives and friends. Ramon greeted each newcomer at the door. The Indians talked and laughed, and then there was a hush. A fire was kindled in the doorway, a small fire of corncobs and paper. The light was taken from the fire in the fireplace, for that fire represented the continuation of the home. Had it gone out by some mischance, it would have to be rekindled from the eternal fire that glowed in the *kiva*. When the little fire in the doorway faded to glowing embers, the mother stepped carefully across it. Then she turned, and threw the fire with a shovel out into the patio. Now, sickness would never follow this baby.

The medicine man of the Red Corn Clan appeared in the doorway. There were six other clans making up the village, but this was the clan of the mother. The mother's sister threw meal on an altar raised in the back of the room, and as she threw the meal she uttered the name "Shiepuyu." The medicine man sprinkled the baby with water from a medicine bowl of pottery, dipped in two duck feathers, and then shook a tiny drop of water into its mouth. From a deerskin sack at his side, he pulled an ear of red corn and gave it to the mother. He breathed out three times and then, taking the corn again, dipped it into the bowl of water and sprinkled the baby again, letting another drop of water fall into its mouth. His services completed, he turned and left the house. The Indians closed around the baby, and she was lifted from her place in front of the altar and passed from one to the other so that all could admire her.

Sunday afternoon the group crowded into the sacristy, where the baptismal font stood. There were two good reasons for the crowd. Here was a new life for the village, which was all important, and here also was added excitement—something to break the routine of living.

Ramon carried the baby proudly, and her long white dress, trimmed with yards of lace, hung in folds to his knees. Father Docher began the prayers and touched the closed lips of the baby with salt. She opened her eyes, licked the salt off, and squirmed at the new sensation. Suddenly Ramon's face clouded, and he passed the baby hurriedly to her mother, muttering, "*Lameda*, Maria, *lameda*." The mother took her and held her up toward the priest, saying softly, "Maria, *lameda*."

A Christening

Father Docher intent on the ritual heard the words objectively. "Maria, lameda." A faint warning clicked in his mind for an instant. Was this the name Ramon had told him? Was this Prayer-Feather-Bright? But the Indian names were slow in coming. His voice rolled deep and sonorous through the sacristy.

"Maria Lameda, I baptize thee, in the name of the Father, and of the Son and of the Holy Ghost. Amen."

There was a deep silence, and he saw the Indians turn puzzled faces toward each other. Suddenly a snicker broke the quietness, and men dashed through the doorway, and he heard their loud laughter as they rolled in the patio.

The mother raised stricken eyes to Tashide. "You have christened the baby Lameda," she gasped. "What a name for a girl-child. But now it is done and nothing can change it. To the Indians she will always be Shiepuyu, Prayer-Feather-Bright, but to the Christian way of thinking she will be called Lameda, Little-Wet-Pants."

10

The Feast of All Souls

OCTOBER was happily slipping away, carrying into the unknown the red of the padre's woodbine and the gold of the river-road cottonwoods, but leaving in the hearts of the Isletans a general feeling of satisfaction. The young bucks had that "plenty-of-corn-in-the-yard" and "chili-on-the-housetops" attitude toward life, and lounged around watching the women and children shucking corn, and sorting the red, the blue, and the black ears into separate piles; stopping to join in the hilarity which greeted a grandmother's pretended wrath when someone threw a worm at her.

The men felt they needed a rest, for the time had been long which they had spent in the fields. According to Valentino the "juice-of-hot" caused by the Sun-Father had brought discomfort to them all, especially during the months of July and August. But all such discomforts were not forgotten, and the old ones said. "Let the wind blow the snow off Shyubato; let it puff and howl all it wants to this winter. We can tell stories of our forefathers and of hunting during the long cold months without fear of the enemy hunger. We will ask the padre to pray that such enemies as 'the-sickness-of-the-sores' and the 'black death' do not visit us. We will be happy."

So young and old stood around taking harvest inventory, occasionally lending a hand in the job of taking down from the housetops the long strings of chili which the October sun had changed from scarlet patent-leatherish peppers into dried and shriveled skins encasing pods of seeds, each pod potent enough to change mutton stew into liquid fire.

The padre thoroughly enjoyed Indian food from afar. Flaming *ristras* of chili fringing white adobes was a sight over which to exclaim, especially when part of the scene was a cobalt sky with

The Feast of All Souls

cloud-galleons slowly riding over a golden sea of cottonwoods, stopping to anchor on towering mountain tops, or sailing far beyond to other ports. But, chili stew was a different matter. He agreed that a seed or two of green or red peppers added dash to frijoles, or mutton stew, but more than a seed or two and the frijoles or mutton had to be washed down with great gulps of water, which was very disturbing indeed. The padre often seriously doubted his psychological approach to digestion, particularly when friends offered him mutton which had been drying on a clothes-line for several weeks, and he happened to know the location of the clothes-line.

As he put on his vestments preparatory to saying Mass on this Holy Day, he knew that most of his flock would be present to offer up the holy sacrifice with him, even though the previous day had been given over to celebrating "the return of their forefathers" in a thoroughly Indian manner. The traditional custom of going up to the housetops and throwing food into the plaza, then very ceremoniously gathering it all up again and putting it into earthen bowls which were later placed on the graves in the little *Campo Santo* adjoining the church, he discouraged heartily. How often during the years he had spent there he had tried to make them understand that the dead relatives and friends needed prayers for the repose of their souls, not food; that the time was gone forever when such things as dried pumpkin seeds, chili, and tortillas could help them. They, year after year, agreed with him solemnly, and then ceremoniously went through the ritual of placing prayer-sticks out near the "Hill-of-the-Wind."

As he entered the sanctuary he noticed that the birds and the beasts, which the mothers yearly made out of the blue cornmeal and placed on the altars in memory of little "Angelitos," were greater in number and variety than formerly. Quite a menagerie in fact! He looked up at the statue of the Blessed Mother, hardly recognizable in her lace-curtain draperies, and he knew that she would understand. So, too, would St. Joseph, the head of the Holy Family, who on that day was almost smothered in pink paper flowers.

In a peacefully reminiscent frame of mind he began to say Mass. The church was cold, and so dark that he had to move a candle, nearer the missal in order to read the prayers. No sounds but the murmur of his voice, the answers of the server, Mariano, and the

The Padre of Isleta

knee-shifting of the worshippers in the pewless old church were heard until the offertory bell tinkled softly. That sound was what probably started the free-for-all barnyard commotion in the holy place. The clarion call of a rooster was joyously acknowledged by the prolonged cackling of hens. In seemingly timed intervals the cluck, clucking was acompanied by the lower tones of the duck. Over all could be heard suppressed but unsuccessful attempts to "shush" giggling children as well as the fowls.

The choral rendition continued intermittently throughout the Mass, but the padre conducted the service with his usual religious, absorption, obviously undisturbed by the uproar. Only Mariano displayed any manifestations of ill-will toward the members of the congregation. Several times he turned around and glared. Faint pencil rays of light filtering in through the high and narrow windows revealed, during a prolonged glare, one who he thought resembled his Uncle Valentino, and what was even worse Uncle Valentino was undoubtedly holding a bird of some variety. He took a good look as he moved the big missal to the Gospel side of the altar. His fears were confirmed. The realization that it was Uncle Valentino caused him to omit the genuflection at the foot of the altar as he changed sides, an omission which bothered him afterwards because the padre himself had trained him. Once Archbishop Chapelle had patted him on the head when he served his Mass, and Father Docher had been pleased.

Now everything was mixed up in his mind. What would the padre say to Uncle Valentino? And what would Uncle Valentino say to the padre? He decided that he would run home right after Mass, and not have breakfast in the priest's house as was the custom on feast days.

But when the padre turned and faced the parishioners and said, *"Ite missa est,"* he spoke out nice and quiet as always. Maybe after all the padre was thankful that it was only chickens and roosters and ducks who disturbed the peace and quiet of that Holy Sacrifice. On other mornings, in other years, so his grandfather had said, Indians had come on the warpath, ready to scalp. High windows and thick walls were constant reminders of marauding Apaches, and warring Navajos. So, things might be worse, Mariano decided, and being thankful that he didn't have to worry about his scalp, he answered

The Feast of All Souls

the final prayers of the Mass with fervor, and walked proudly by the padre's side out to the sacristy, wishing that his surplice had more lace on it.

Valentino headed the procession which filed into the sacristy after them and into the room where Father Docher was disrobing. The leader clutched a big rooster. Dolores followed close behind, holding two fat Rhode Island Reds, and Ysidro, her husband, had a very nice young turkey. The others, closely scrutinizing the face of the padre, had pumpkins, sacks of grain, lard buckets filled with beans, and strings of the prized blue and red ears of maize.

Valentino's jet-black hair was confined by a gay silk handkerchief, jauntily knotted in the back. His large silver earrings dangled as he seriously explained. "Because this is the Feast of All Souls, we have brought you gifts for the saying of masses for the souls of the dead. You know, Padre, the 'responsas.' We have had a good year, so the chickens and roosters are special." There was only a short pause. It was as Mariano hoped; the priest smiled, Valentino shifted the rooster, and the procession moved across the patio to the kitchen.

Suddenly in through the gate rushed a troop of laughing children swinging flour sacks and singing at the top of their voices the traditional song:

> *"Hear us! Hear us! Little angels are we,*
>
> *Who from heaven have come to ask for alms,*
>
> *And if we are denied,*
>
> *Doors and windows we will break!*
>
> *Hear us! Hear Us!"*

All present joined in the song as the padre began to fill the sacks from the harvest gifts just presented to him. That is, all but Valentino, who the padre noted out of the corner of his eye was looking glum, and slowly edging away. But he need not have worried. He had no intention of offending Valentino. With a little garlic, that old rooster would make a very nice festival dish.

II

El Padre Sargento

"Why don't you want the railroad to come through the fields?" the padre asked a delegation of his Indian friends sitting in his study late one day in July of 1902.

Valentino looked around the roomful of people and said sullenly, "We don't want it to cross the fields. Also it makes too much noise so close to us. It scares the women and children. We will get ready to fight."

"You fought once before, Valentino," the padre said, looking at him. But at this point in the arranged meeting, Valentino became interested in adjusting the many strands of turquoise beads he had on for the occasion, separating them from the coral necklaces which vied in lustre with Valentino's coal-black hair.

But the padre had no intention of recalling to the assembled group of Indians and railroad representatives Valentino's share in allowing a railroad official, sent to Isleta some weeks before for the purpose of discussing the proposed right-of-way, to be locked in jail. Only the pleas of the padre, and Valentino's obviously sincere promises of better behavior, had saved the latter from finding himself locked in the one-room village jail.

After his open declaration against the railroad on this particular afternoon, the men of the village listened in silence to the lawyers' proposal of ample compensation for the right-of-way through the reservation, but they gave no sign of interest. Not a head moved when they heard the official announcement that the people of Isleta would receive "free rides" on the train, and they all seemed to be engrossed in watching a green bottlefly buzzing around the head of the lawyer, rather than in his statement that there was possibility of the people of Isleta making some money out of the plan. "In the

El Padre Sargento

winter," said the white man, "you can sell your pottery and rings to the tourists who may stop over in the pueblo, and in the summer you may sell some of your fruit."

Concernedly the padre looked at the Indians through the long afternoon; noting how guileless they looked in summer pants made of flour sacks, and muslin shirts with crochet lace-fronts of intricate flower and animal designs. The lawyers from Albuquerque looked at them concernedly, too, but they noted the strength of jaw and limb, and tried to read consent to the ways of progress in the expressionless faces of men who wore earrings.

The pueblo delegation had looked at each other at the conclusion of the speech-making. Nothing was said, and nothing was heard but the drone of bees in the patio and the sputtering of the red votive lamp in front of a statue of the Blessed Virgin. Finally, Valentino rose slowly from his place in front of the Indians, and crossing the space which separated the foes from the friends, very solemnly shook the hand of the lawyer, and then, turning to Father Docher said, with a gesture of acceptance, "We have decided. Let the railroad come."

Shortly afterwards work was begun on the project which was to establish a more direct route for the Santa Fe Railroad. The villagers took on an air of importance as they watched the gangs of laborers, and laughingly asked the padre to explain the job of the man who stood in the middle of the fields squinting through a thing that stood on three poles.

The laughter changed to sullen resentment as they noted what happened when the high grade for the railroad was completed. "The corn and the chili will be ruined," Valentino said in an ugly mood to the padre one night, as the two of them stood looking at the embankment which divided the great field lying north of the village, and dammed the water in the irrigation ditches. The padre tried to explain that new ditches would have to be made, but Valentino made no answer. He stood looking at the ties which had arrived that morning.

The following afternoon, as the priest sat in his study writing some long over-due letters, he heard the voice of Teresita Sandoval, his nearest neighbor, directing her daughters in the manner and art of plastering. The back-breaking job of covering the earth-born

The Padre of Isleta

adobes was traditionally done by the women in July, the month which always found the children sensibly wading in the *acequias,* or gathering cat-tails down by the river. The men squatted against the adobe walls, singly or in groups, and chaffed the sweating wives and mothers, complimenting them on their grace in carrying buckets of mortar up ladders, or their deftness in wielding a trowel.

Suddenly the drifting voices changed into jig-saw yells and shrieks, momentarily heightened by barking dogs and running feet. The padre, fearing an accident, hastened out to the plaza with his dog at his heels. Relieved, he heartily joined in the fun when he arrived on the scene and found out the cause of the uproar.

There on the flat roof of the Sandoval house stood Teresita furiously battling with a swarm of bees which she had dislodged from an age-old corner *viga,* punctuating each swish of her bright red shawl with a yell to her daughters, who seemed to be successfully dodging the rapidly increasing swarm and thoroughly enjoying the concerted attack on their mother. Advice was freely flowing from the assembled crowd below, but Teresita wisely decided to call a halt to the plastering. Ordering her daughters to withdraw, she hastily grabbed her bucket of mortar and led the way down the ladder to receive the sympathy of her friends and exhibit the battle-scars.

As the padre stood on the outskirts of the crowd enjoying the excitement, it suddenly occurred to him as he looked around that there was not a man there. Still wondering about their absence, as he turned to go back to his interrupted letter writing, he met Maria and asked her where the men were. Maria made no answer, but lowered her eyes and turned away. The priest slowly walked on, for he knew as well as if she had told him that they were gathered together in the kiva. He remembered Valentino's face as he looked at the railroad ties, and he knew that the time for counseling was over. He, too, would have to make ready for action.

That night Father Docher prayed for his children as he walked alone in the darkness to the outskirts of the pueblo. High over the "Hill-of-the-Wind" hung a star, and far to the east loomed the Manzanos, dark and forbidding. There, where the embankment crossed the main fields, the padre saw the men, as he had expected. He quickened his pace, and walked among them for a few minutes

El Padre Sargento

unrecognized, looking for Valentino, whom he had heard giving the men directions. They were just as he had feared; the embankment was to be leveled, and all the railroad ties were to be destroyed. The honor of the people of Isleta would be gone by morning.

Stepping up to the leader, the priest called aloud in a voice never heard before in the pueblo, "You must not do this! You do not realize what it is you do!"

But Valentino came forward and belligerently replied, "I am in charge of the village. We will do as we wish. It is none of your business." His words grew in ugliness as the message was passed through the crowd of Indians now closing in to the side of their leader. Then "El Padre Sargento" quietly pulled a gun from his pocket and pointed it straight at Valentino.

High over "Eagle Feather Mountain" the moon "walked," silvering the valley and showing the men of Isleta a stranger standing there before them. Gone were the ways of the old friend and compadre. In his place stood the soldier of whom they had heard; one who had won medals for bravery. Once more he spoke, but quietly this time. "You will go back to your homes. I have come for you."

Slowly the tension broke, the men fell back, and the padre put the unloaded gun back in his pocket. Valentino stepped to the side of the soldier-priest. "We will do as you wish," he said. And together they led the men back to the village.

The pattern of life in Isleta flowed on with the cycle of seasons unchanged by the monster who daily roared by. Often the men stopped their work in the fields to listen to the shriek of the whistle far off in the distance, or to wave at the trainmen and passengers. Many of them had gone for the "free rides," which the padre heard they enjoyed.

One day the following summer, as he was cleaning out his well in the back garden, the martial-minded Valentino came in. There was a new sort of worry in his eyes and the padre was sorry because he thought that his troubles were over. Valentino helped with the cleaning job, and when they had finished said, as he twirled his sombrero, "Tashide, I am having trouble with Maria. Always she wants to go on the 'free rides.' She stayed two days in Belen last week. Then she came home with shoes with heels and hats with flowers. The people are laughing, and I have talked with my friends.

The Padre of Isleta

We have decided that the 'free rides' should be given to others. Let the people of Laguna have them."

The padre slowly shook his head and agreed that the dangers were many, and he promised to do what he could in the serious matter before them. Valentino then gratefully shook the hand of his sympathizer, who smiled as the guest turned to take his departure. Across the seat of the traditional flour-sack pants worn by Valentino was clearly discernible the brand of a well-known flour with the motto, "For Family Use." Several hard scrubbings on the part of Maria might restore the dignity of Valentino, but just at present her interests were obviously elsewhere.

12

The Witch

FATHER DOCHER sat with his broad shoulders against the wall of the church watching the people swarm into the plaza. His grey eyes squinted in the sunlight as he considered this phenomenon of these people who were Christians, sincerely and truthfully, as Bandelier had told him, and yet just as sincerely and truthfully practiced the rites of their nature religion. It was March, and the Indians were dancing the Twia-Fu-Wide, the dance of the Dark Katchina, asking Those Above for good spring and crops.

There had been a four-day retreat to the kiva and the moiety chiefs had gone at three in the morning to the corners of the plaza, calling the young men to ride forth to Eagle Feather mountain, where the White Katchina lived. They went on horseback to find green spruce for the ritual. There in the mountains they would leave prayer sticks, tipped with the feathers of the bluebird. And now they would leave candles side by side with the prayer-feather-sticks.

The women had swept all of the yards in the village clean, and they had cleared a path down to the river. At mid-morning a messenger brought word that the men were returning from the mountains, and all of those of the village went to the river to meet them. The young men leaped into the river, forded it, and came into the plaza with their clothes dripping. Rushing to the huge bonfire in the middle of the plaza, they pulled off their wet clothes and dried them, and then ran around among the people making jokes for laughter. One of the young men came before the padre, stroked his beard in friendliness, and then knelt for his blessing. This act to a stranger might mean disrespect to the man of the church, but to Father Docher it was the expression of the spirit of fellowship and trust.

He felt a slight tug at his arm and turned to find Dolores standing beside him. Her face drooped in contrast to those laughing about him.

"Tashide, I must speak with you. There are too many people here."

"We will go to my study, Dolores. I think I have some peacook feathers for your two children." They passed through the crowd, and one of the madcap boys shouted, "Dolores, the goats dance, and the bats fly."

Dolores hunched her blanket more tightly about her shoulders. "Listen, Father, the people of the village are laughing."

In the study, she pushed back her blanket and toyed with the peacock feathers he had given her.

"Last night Jose was gone again from our blankets. He is bewitched by Manuelita. Why, he often meets her in the dark of the evening at one of the four heaps of refuse, those that are piled on the four sides of the village. That is where the witches bury their bundles."

Tashide shook his head gravely. "To talk of witches is serious, Dolores; and for you to call Manuelita a witch—that is a very serious charge."

"She never goes out in the daytime, Father," responded Dolores by way of explanation. "All of her work is done in the night-time. She stays out until cockcrow and then rushes home to her house and closes the door."

"But a witch, Dolores—that is something difficult to handle."

"Yes, Tashide, so you tell us; but even Lummis was bewitched. You know yourself he couldn't lift his arm until the white doctors broke the spell.

"And, as for Manuelita, well, once two years ago, I went out with her. That was against the wishes of my parents. But she said we would go to a feast. We left the village and went far out on the mesa. We came to a house sitting alone. It was dark, but we heard drumming. She knocked at the door. Inside were people, Spanish people from Los Lunas, dancing and laughing. They danced and they sang, and suddenly I saw a goat dancing among them. I looked at Manuelita. Her feet had turned to hooves and then I knew that I was in a witch's gathering. I knew I would be bewitched. I pushed against the door, but it was fastened and then I held to this cross on

The Witch

my neck and prayed, 'Virgin Purissima,' and, Father, she saved me from them; for I pushed on the door again and it opened."

Dolores settled herself more firmly in the chair and continued with a recital of her grievances. She looked carefully at Father Docher to see the effect of her story on him. He was staring out of the window and drumming with his right hand on the arm of the chair.

"I could go to some witch out of our village, for, of course, those out of the village work stronger spells than those who live here. Now, at Sandia pueblo," she began speculatively, "those witches are strong. But, Father, you can help me. Last night I started to see you, but I knew I shouldn't venture out after sundown or the witches would catch me. Just as I came to the corral behind the church, I heard loud footsteps behind me. There came a breathing over my shoulder and I couldn't turn to see what was following me. I had to stand there until dawn, because my feet would not move." She leaned back exhausted with the great injustice that had been done to her.

"Jose wears a hat that Manuelita gave him. I know that just as long as he wears it he will go to her. Once I took it and he beat me. Now, of an evening, he puts it on and says that he is going to the *kiva*." Her face drew in scorn as she thought of the lie he had told her. "He tells me that he goes there to feed the Navajo scalps that are hidden in the wall, because that will cure the toothache. Of curse, feeding the scalps will cure the toothache, but his teeth seem to hurt him all the time. And, anyway," she shifted again in the chair and readjusted her blanket around her shoulders, "every Indian in Isleta knows very well that a woman has to feed the scalps all the time; for if a man feeds them, the ghost of the dead Navajo will come back with a rope around his neck and he will cry and moan through the village."

Father Docher remembered one of the first discussions he had with Bandelier about religion and the belief in witches. And he remembered, too, the story that Ramon had told him—the struggle between the Christian belief and the Indian belief.

"Look, Father, at that fly on the window. Is it not strange for a fly to be here in March? It is early for flies—that means someone is coming. Maybe you will have news for me, for my eye twitched when I first came into the study."

The Padre of Isleta

"Yes, Dolores, someone is coming. I want you to go home and tell Jose to come here and talk with me. Then I shall have news for you. But, this is important. After you have talked to Jose, I want you to pray to the Blessed Mother."

Dolores looked slightly disappointed. "But the hat. Manuelita is a witch, I know it. She goes to Shimtua, the cave, five miles to the southwest. That is where the witches gather." She looked hopefully at him, but seeing only calmness in his face, she pulled her blanket over her head and picked up the peacock feathers. "Very well, I will pray; but the hat—"

The rest of her thoughts on the hat were lost in the March sunshine.

Out in the plaza the Indians continued their dancing. That afternoon Jose called at the study. He seemed slightly nervous and hesitant. He was obviously prepared to defend himself if necessary. But Father Docher talked with him at great length of planting time in the village and of hunting. He was interested in the fact that though many of the Indians used arrows in hunting, and rabbit sticks in killing the rabbits, many more were using guns. He mentioned some who were practicing with new guns.

Jose left sometime later with an expression of thoughtfulness on his face. Nothing had been said about his family troubles.

Dolores came back that evening, just as the dancing was over. "Tashide, I prayed as you told me to, and my prayers were answered. As Jose came home a gust of wind caught off his hat and carried it across the mesa. Now that it is gone, the witch's spell is broken. Jose said that his teeth ached no more, and he will not feed the Navajo scalps as he has been doing."

As Father Docher watched her pass through the patio gate, he knew that her faith was stronger in the efficacy of Christian prayer. He smiled and shook his head, and asked for forgiveness from the Holy Mother. For through him, Jose had learned that Manuelita's husband was the possessor of a new gun; that, as a target, he had been using an old hat he had found in the trash heap; and that accidents in shooting with new guns sometimes happen in Indian villages.

13

El Santo Niño

THE summers of the years were hot and unvaryingly the same. Every August the heat hung over the village like a suffocating white blanket. Then Father Docher stayed much of his time in the cool adobe study. The Indians sought him for talk and advice on many of their troubles. Their troubles usually resolved themselves into episodes, at times disheartening to the priest in their outcome. But, somehow, so strange is life, each episode though complete within itself seemed to fit eventually into the next one, making of life a wholeness and a completeness. The experience with the statues of Saint Augustine had been such an episode.

The little, wooden, two-foot high statue of Saint Augustine stood on the altar—hand-carved, with black beard, tonsured head, robes decorated in figured gold—old and softened by time. It had been brought back up the long road from the South when the Indians had returned after the rebellion of 1680. The Isletans always addressed personal petitions, as well as affairs that concerned the village, directly to the Saint, feeling confident that some satisfaction would be derived from their petitions.

Soon after his arrival in the village, Father Docher had ordered a new statue. It was tall and beautifully colored in the French manner—blue and gold. He was sure that the Indians would like its shining brightness on the altar. After its arrival he went to the church the following Sunday to celebrate Mass, and noted with interest that the people gazed respectfully at the new Saint Augustine, gleaming from the altar. But, as time slipped by, the padre realized the offerings of beads of red coral continued to be made to the old Saint Augustine, who stood unobtrusively on the left of the altar.

The following April of that year so long gone by, a delegation of towns-people came and asked that they be permitted to take Saint

The Padre of Isleta

Augustine, the elder, on the usual trip around the fields, so that he would understand their need for rain during the summer. Saint Augustine, the younger, had been completely ignored. When Father Docher had asked Emeliano about the preference, Emeliano had answered, with a characteristic shrug of his shoulders, "Well, Saint Augustine, the old one, always has been our friend. What if he is old and ugly? The medicine men are old—but wise through experience." And with another shrug Emeliano had left this bit of Indian philosophy to the then young priest.

This August the dryness perplexed the people, for they must have rains or the crops would not grow. Each day the hot rays of the sun pierced into every opening. Doors and windows were closed. The white walls of the houses and the church threw back the heat waves which beat with renewed vigor on the plaza, until it seemed a white dead thing. The very dogs of the village lay lifeless in thin strips of black, and in the corrals the horses stood with hanging heads. Even the roosters neglected to crow, and the hens pecked listlessly in the frayed shade. Out in the fields the young corn drooped, and an occasional lost little wind caused the stalks to rustle dryly. The edges of the chili leaves crisped and their gloss grew dull and grey. The thin thread of the river trickled thinner. Even the great cottonwoods that rimmed the river bent lower and spread wide, seeming to protect the thinning thread from the sun's drinking rays.

The faces of those of Isleta had grown strained, and Father Docher too shared the tenseness that drew the village. Each morning he prayed for relief. The women passed from the well with *ollas* of water balanced on their heads, their white moccasined feet hurrying them to the shade of their own houses. The old men had gathered at night in their *kivas* and debated about their greatest enemy—for no rain meant the crops would not bear and then there would be tragedy and death stalking the village.

Even in the cool shaded patio that the priest tended with such care, the roses were drooping and the parrots sat silently on their perches. The peacocks were quiet and their gorgeous tails lay in the dust.

In the New Mexico summer the drought often lasted the season; but not always for sometimes in the greatest heat, clouds would gather over the Manzano Mountains in the distance, and the earth would remain quiet in waiting. Then the clouds traveled swiftly and

View of Isleta.

El Santo Nino

folded over the waiting land. The rain would sweep in grey sheets on the parched fields and dry rivers—great cloudbursts—water released by the sudden contact of the dry heat waves with the sodden clouds. Usually such a cloudburst lasted for several minutes and then stopped; but there were times when heavy rains came, lasting for several days.

The ringing of the bell on the patio gate interrupted Father Docher in his musings and his memories. As he walked through the patio to receive his callers, he felt the great quietness of the village. That was strange. For eleven days there had been the pulsing throb of drums. The town chief, and the *kaan,* the medicine men of fire, had been in retreat in the *kiva*. In order that their gods would heed them, they had fasted. On their altar terraced clouds had been designed in white meal of the corn. There too had been a bowl of medicine water, fetish stones, arrow points, bear claws, and prayer feathers from the sparrow hawk.

For the past three days no smoke had risen from the village. The town chief, the evening before, had proceeded with the ritual of lighting with a flint the hollow reeds gathered from the riverside and packed with dried mullen leaves. The first six puffs by each smoker were ceremoniously offered to the East, to the West, to the North, to the South, to Those Above, and to Those Below. Tonight, the twelfth, all of the old men of the tribe had been there. Lightning had darted around the walls, and thunder had rocked the altar on which was placed the sacred, fetishistic, cotton-wrapped mother-corn. How the thunder came into the kiva or why the lightning flashed, no one knew except the medicine men. But they all knew that by the Indian ritual, the drought should be broken.

On this morning after the ritual, the sun seemed closer to the earth. No clouds were seen gathering. Nothing indicated that Those Above had heard. Now, in the mid-morning heat, Father Docher greeted four old men of the tribe. Inside the study, the Indians ranged themselves around the floor, leaning against the walls. They talked little—only sat in that comfortable silence that means understanding. Ramon, glancing at his companions, spat reflectively. "We men of the tribe have talked," he said. "We have thought more."

The priest said nothing. He knew that waiting was the best in times like these and so they sat while the shadows lengthened and

The Padre of Isleta

the breath of evening coolness came. Father Docher stirred in his chair, and then Emeliano spoke.

"Tashide, you told us once that *El Santo Nino*, the Holy Child, would help us in times of trouble." The priest nodded. "Tomorrow after the Mass is said, we would like a procession with the Child. True, we usually take Saint Augustine to help us in times of drought, but this is very bad. We have decided that we will carry *El Santo Niño* to our parched and dying fields, and when he sees with his own eyes that unless there is rain we will die, it may be that he will make the rain." All of the men in the room looked at the priest, in their eyes the question—could he help them?

The padre arose and the wrinkles around his grey eyes clustered as he smiled. "Tell the people to come to Mass in the morning. We will pray for rain and then we will have a procession made up of all the people in the village."

The next morning there was a steady flow of people into the church. Everyone knew that the *Santo Niño* was to be taken from the church. Long before the bells finished clanging for Mass, every person in the village was in the church. Some leaned against the walls—many prayed, and as they prayed they studied the small figure of the Child held in the arms of the Virgin. After Mass four women came to the sanctuary for *el palio*. Father Docher placed the figure of the Child carefully upon it. The Indians drew back on each side, forming a clear passageway for the priest as he passed, followed by the women, in their bright blankets, carrying the statue. Then, chanting prayers, they all closed in, forming the procession.

Back of the church they wended their way down to the fields. At the railway crossing the priest turned back, but the procession marched on. Bright blankets glowed in the sun, and moccasined feet raised the fine dust in a choking cloud. A baby coughed and then cried, a thin noise above the swish of moccasined feet in the dust, and the monotone of the chant of prayers.

As the procession drew near the first field, the glare of the sun faded and a shadow fell. The Indians raised their eyes and there to the east, over the trees, over Eagle Feather mountain, lay a thunder cloud. It grew as they watched, and turned blacker and blacker. Before the first field had been circled, the tiny drops fell, and then with a roar came the rain. The people laughed as they pulled their

El Santo Niño

drenched blankets about them. Children leaped in the rain, and the church bell rang out through the storm. The Christ Child had heard them; the Christ Child had helped them.

All that night the rain poured. The next morning the grey skies drooped in a drizzle, the water roared down the river, and the trees lifted their branches. Out in the fields the corn stood straight and the leaves of the chili plants glistened. At noon the rain came harder, and by night water ran through the roads and feet sloshed in the mud. The horses stood dejectedly in their corrals with their backs turned against the rain; the dogs hugged tightly to the houses; the corn drooped again, but now from the water-soaked earth, and the chili plants lay sprawled in the mud. For three days and nights there was rain and hail; the river roared by, eating out the irrigation ditches. The roots of cottonwood trees lay exposed as the river banks caved in.

Father Docher shook his head in anxiety over the summer floods. On the afternoon of the third day, he heard the shuffling of feet in his patio and there stood the same four friends who had come to him before. Again they entered; again they ranged themselves around the wall of the room, silently watching the rain on the window; again Emeliano spoke.

"Tashide," he said, "four days ago we came to you seeking protection. We asked aid of the *Santo Niño*. We showed him our fields, our wilted corn, our chili. We asked him to send us rain so that we would not die. And what did he do?"

Father Docher did not answer, he merely waited for Emeliano to continue.

"What did he do? He sent floods." All of the men nodded. "Now," Emeliano said, "we have talked this over; our crops will be ruined unless the rain ceases. We have decided there should be another procession. This time we will take the Blessed Virgin and show her what her child has done."

A silver splinter of sun suddenly cut through the room, and through the windows they saw the sun breaking through the clouds. They looked at one another and sighed in relief, and the Padre joined the sigh audibly.

"Well," said Emeliano, "we won't need to take the Virgin in a procession; she has already heard us. So it is with children, even the Holy Child, he went too far."

And once again they filed from the study, leaving Tashide to ponder again the strange episodes that make up the life of a missionary.

14

Justice Is Administered

THE wind gave no indication of letting up on its obviously preordained mission of removing all the sand from the eastern foot-hills and mesa over to the western foot-hills and mesa. Enough sand to fill a giant salt and pepper shaker had sifted into his eyes, ears, nose and lungs, the padre decided one late March night as he was returning from Peralta, a little Spanish settlement south of Isleta, and a part of his Mission. He had been called there to administer the Last Sacrament to Manuela Chavez, the *"mamacita,"* as she was lovingly called up and down the valley. This marked the third time he had given her Extreme Unction, but each time she had returned from her *Jornada del Muerto* to welcome and bless a new great-grandchild.

Some said she was a hundred and four years old, and as the priest lighted the Blessed Candle to guide her on her way, he was convinced that the corporal and spiritual works of mercy she had performed in this desert and mountainous country during her unnumbered years would admit her straight into heaven. Certainly she would receive a joyous reception from the many missionaries whose hardships she had lightened through those years, especially for the help she had given in teaching classes in the catechism, and in preparing the children for their First Holy Communion . . . In his own experience he knew of many little girls whose white dresses for the beautiful occasion had been made by the *mamacita*.

The rambling old Chavez adobe surrounded by cottonwoods, giants of a river-road of time, held many treasures from Mexico and Spain, the gifts of grateful travelers along the "King's Highway." The most treasured of all was a silver crucifix, which, according to legend, had once belonged to Coronado. It hung in a special niche, a piece of exquisite workmanship and a constant reminder of sacrifice.

The Padre of Isleta

Her children did not inherit her characteristics, the padre reflected, as he looked at Ambrosio, her eldest son, sitting near the foot of the bed vainly trying to wrap his tongue around a last tooth.

"About how old is your mother?" Father Docher had asked. And Ambrosio had looked far off, searched bewildered through his world of legend and fact for a long time, and then had answered "She was born the time smoke was seen coming out of the big volcano." As the padre turned to give the dying woman a final blessing, he included Ambrosio, who he felt was the one who needed it.

The wind was continuing to come from every direction, hitting the buggy-top with insistent hammerings. He didn't know how it could stand many more such "lambastings," and he also didn't know where the money would come from for a new one . . . He decided right then to begin concentrating on St. Jude, "dispenser of favors." He made an attempt to get some of the sand out of his mouth before beginning to hum the Litany of the Blessed Virgin, but it was a futile effort, and he was forced to stop for a few minutes in order to wipe the sand-saliva mixture which had landed back on his face. He wondered if the Lord provided some sort of an anatomical repository for the grit which humans swallowed in such storms, and smilingly recalled the concern of the Le Crest doctors over his weak lungs. But that was of the past, of time long gone in his life. So he slapped the reins on the back of his pinto and yelled a word of encouragement at the top of those once weak lungs to the horse "Old-Man-Afraid-of-the-Water," as the Indians called him. He was so named because when they were both new to the country, and not yet weather-broken, a tiny trickle of water in the bottom of an arroyo stretching across the road had suddenly become a towering wall of water. Both priest and pinto after floundering desperately had finally gotten across the arroyo, but the buggy had been whirled down the muddish-red flood. He had learned a lesson, however, and many times since then, he had read his Office as he waited for Old-Man-Afraid-of-the-Water to pass judgment on a stream trickling slowly across the road during the rainy season.

The job ahead of them on this particular night was to get across the narrow wooden bridge which spanned the river between Isleta and Peralta. Old-Man-Afraid-of-the-Water made it more by the grace of God than by horse sense. The middle hazard of the bridge,

Justice Is Administered

some always-loose boards, was overlooked in the excitement of seeing a light ahead in the distance. "Some *paisano* lost in the storm," he explained to the pinto. "He will be disappointed when he finds out that we are almost home."

When they stopped, the padre immediately recognized Vicente's new sombrero in the feeble lantern light. Vicente himself was hardly recognizable in a Navajo blanket with which he was having a great deal of difficulty, and a bandana handkerchief tied tightly across his mouth. The Indian friend would probably offer no explanation of his appearance there until they were sharing a cup of warmed over Arbuckle's in the padre's kitchen. Although the priest respected his friend's silent approach to confidence, such a meeting bordered on the sensational, and he began to check over the Governor's official duties in preparation for emergency advice after Vicente had climbed into the buggy, satisfactorily wrapped his blanket around himself, tied the bandana tighter, and pulled the new hat down to his eyes.

But he could not arrive at a solution. Since the inaugural ceremony, Vicente had been carefully attending to his many duties as governor. In accepting the padre's congratulations at that time, Vicente had said, "I want no one to say when I surrender the Lincoln Cane of Authority, that I failed to lead the Sun People, the Earth People, the Water-Pebble People, the Eagle People, the Mole People, the Antelope People, the Deer People, the Mountain-Lion People, the Turquoise People, the Parrot People, the White Corn People, the Red Corn People, the Blue Corn People, the Yellow Corn People, the Goose People, or the Wolf People in the right direction." And as far as the padre's knowledge was concerned all members of the sixteen clans were cooperating to make Vicente's period of office a happy and successful one.

The two friends covered the remaining distance in conversationless silence which was broken, as the padre had anticipated, over coffee and a rolled cigarette, and then with official gravity.

"Padre, did you see anything of Pedro Lucero in Peralta?" Vicente inquired.

"You mean Juan Biscocho's cousin?" The padre replied as he shook his head negatively.

"'The man has been gone three days, presumably looking for a

The Padre of Isleta

horse in that direction," explained Vicente. "His wife Mercedes just came to tell me tonight. She should have come sooner. We fear that he has been killed."

The priest knew Pedro Lucero as a responsible husband and father, but a three-day horse-hunting expedition was not of sufficient seriousness in such a large pueblo as Isleta to keep the tired missionary's head from frequent and prolonged nods. No doubt Pedro had found the horse and had gone visiting on it. But Vicente interpreted the nods as agreement to his plan to put the Town Crier, the War Captain, the First and Second Lieutenant-Governors, and the two sheriffs on the job of hunting for the missing Isletan, after consulting of course, the *cacique* and the Business Council of Twelve.

If Father Docher, or any one else, had any doubts regarding the governor's executive ability, or the seriousness of Pedro's disappearance from the pueblo, all such doubts were dispelled the following day upon hearing the Town Crier after Vespers announce from the housetop the first official bulletin to the effect that "some boys had seen Pedro and another man riding on one horse three days ago."

Friends of Pedro looked gloomy. Only fleeting glimpses of Vicente were caught as he disappeared into the *estufa,* or galloped off toward the south in search of clews. A week passed. Then one day the tension broke with the announcement that the governor had found the one who had been riding with Pedro. "It was Juan Montoya, but he could not be put in jail because he had ridden with his friend only a short time."

Then reports began to trickle in by way of kitchen—and the general store, that Juan Montoya was always down by the river bridge looking at the water in a very suspicious manner.

In spite of Father Docher's conviction that the *mamacita* would die the night he had been called to give her the Last Sacrament, she had lingered on, and it was two weeks later that he was called to say her Funeral Mass. He took Esteban with him to serve, slightly disappointed that he could not wear his red cassock, because *mamacita* had made it for his Uncle Pablo. The padre felt that it would not be hard to accept such a traditional theory in regard to the original owner, judging by the looks of the robe.

As they crossed the bridge, the padre noted with interest that

Justice Is Administered

several surveyors were working along the river bank. For some months there had been talk of a new bridge and because he recognized in the workmen a symbol, at least, of protest against sudden, unprovided death, he heartily joined in with Esteban's shouted *"Como le va."*

All of Doña Chavez' contemporaries had long since preceded her to the *Campo Santo* adjoining the Peralta church, where the funeral procession slowly walked after the Requiem High Mass, but it was filled with relatives and friends of later generations. The bright sunlight of early spring filtered through lavender-plumed tamarisk trees, making fringed shadows near the new grave. Meadow-larks flitting from juniper bushes on the surrounding hills, the murmured prayers of Father Docher, and the sniffling of Ambrosio, were the only sounds which broke the eternal silence spreading out in ever-widening spaces from the little cemetery, far across the mesa to the cloud-shadowed Manzanos beyond.

Priest and server left for the Indian pueblo in a happier frame of mind after several cups of strong coffee and some lamb stew, mingled with assurances from all the children that they were not forgetting to say their morning and evening prayers.

No sign of life was seen on the way home but a few lizards which Esteban, as he proudly drove along, startled into great activity by a flick of the whip. Both man and boy jogging along through the wasteland, knew, however, that near the banks of the river the willow-barks were turning red, *acequias* were running full, and the rich, brown earth was being plowed and prepared for growth and life.

The padre, intent on developing the thoughts, emotions and reflections of the morning into a little sermon on life, death, growth and decay, was startled out of his contemplative reverie by a yell from Esteban. "Look, padre," he cried, pointing the whip at a crowd of men standing on the opposite side of the bridge which they had neared.

As the priest had somehow expected, there stood Vicente in the center of the group and standing with him were the other officials of the village, and the surveyors. But this time the governor's stoicism was gone, and the padre, following his excited steps to the canvas-covered object lying on the ground, was shocked to hear him say,

The Padre of Isleta

"It is the body of Pedro Lucero. The white men found it in the river this morning. His head was smashed, and his hands and feet tied. We will have to lock up Juan Montoya again. I think he is the one who had something to do with Pedro's death."

And so Juan Montoya was jailed again, but the mystery of Pedro's death was buried in a silence which extended through the days, weeks and months, to be broken only once before it extended through the years. One morning as Father Docher was crossing the plaza he saw Vicente supervising a number of men, cleaning it. The new sombrero presented to him when elected was now slightly battered, but red flannels, visible through white crochet shirt front, defied the July heat which hung over the village and beat against the white adobe walls only to be thrust back in scorn into the hard and cracked ground of the plaza.

They talked of old Maria who sat day after day on the northeast corner of the plaza, lifting sightless eyes to passers-by, of the grasshoppers that threatened ruin to the fields, and of the coming *fiesta*. Then, as the padre turned to leave, Vicente with a jerk of his head towards Juan Montoya, busily sweeping, "You see we let him out of jail. Some one has to support Pedro's family. We might just as well let Juan do it."

15

Archbishop Chapelle Is Welcomed

"You have done quite well with your garden," said Father Henri as he took another bite out of a hard little green pear. "How many years is it now that you have been in Isleta?" he asked, spitting out a wormy piece and looking playfully disgusted at Father Joubert, who made the third of a trio of missionaries sitting in Father Docher's patio one afternoon in late August.

"Fifteen years," replied the padre of Isleta, picking up the wormy piece and throwing it to the peacock that was proudly flaunting its green and gold fan for the benefit of the visitors from Tomé and Laguna.

"Remember the hills of Chambourcy, sloping down to the Seine, and the miles of trellised pear trees, trained *en espalier* for generations?" continued the man who for the past fifteen years had lived in an isolated Indian pueblo. "I wonder if the peasants still tie each pear in a paper sack in order to preserve it from the birds."

"I have no difficulty with birds," said Father Docher, looking upward to watch a flock of wild ducks as they sailed from the north. "Let's suggest to the Archbishop that he mission Father Docher to Tomé. My gourd vines aren't doing very well," said Father Joubert, looking appreciatively at the patio enclosed on the west by the church, the buttressed walls of which were casting long shadows across the garden. To the north and east the four-foot adobe wall enclosed the garden, and to the south stretched the rambling old *Convento* through whose open doorways and windows one could see glimpses of the orchard where grew the hard little pears and even harder cling-stone peaches.

"I thought his Grace was going to discuss the possibility of making you the new Vicar-General," teased the host of the day.

"No, I know a better man," replied the writer of a Navajo

The Padre of Isleta

dictionary, who was to spend the next twenty years of his life in the wind-swept town of Las Vegas, "and, what is more to the point, we haven't said our Office for the day as yet. I am on my way to meditate in the church."

"I will join you," said Father Henri, rising at the same time. "There are too many distractions out here."

This pious announcement was followed by a series of raucous yells, and the two priests turning to see from whence came the derisive laughter saw that Tina, the padre's parrot, dumbly swinging in her cage, was up to her old tricks.

"I thought you didn't have any trouble with birds," laughed the old friend from Laguna.

"I don't," replied Father Docher, "but guests sometimes annoy her." He looked at the parrot, who on meeting his stare called forth gayly, "Buenos dias." "Su gracia." "Ave Maria." "Purissima."

The two men bowed gayly in return, as the padre murmured apologetically but quite proudly, "Just a case of mistaken identity, but you will agree that she has improved."

Both the priests knew Tina, the gift of a passing tourist, and they also knew that if one judged the parrot by the extent and variety of her vocabulary one would surmise that she had not always graced a missionary's garden. Her past was her own, but her linguistic abilities were known from Taos to Acoma. Not many could follow the sophisticated bird's swift sallies into unknown fields of language, or fathom her seaman's epithets done with a Spanish twist. Archbishop Chapelle, on the occasion of his last visit, had diplomatically remarked, after a vituperative outburst, that the parrot's enunciation was not always clear. Father Docher had regretfully agreed, but blamed the fact on her gutterals.

So, in the ensuing months, the reform program as inaugurated by the padre began to show shape and design, and the parrot began to take on the most saintly of ways. She seemed to glory in at least the sound of her new vocabulary, and trilled so nicely over such words as "Ave Maria, Purissima," that the backdrop of her life seemed blotted out and new pattern lay before her.

On this particular day the padre gave her a broad wink of encouragement, perfectly confident of her future good behavior, as the priests dispersed to comply with a religious duty before the arrival

Archbishop Chapelle Is Welcomed

of the distinguished guest, momentarily expected from Santa Fe.

Looking after the two friends and then at his garden, Father Docher mentally agreed with them that one could not give his thoughts wholly to God in this place; but he concluded, as with prayer book in hand, he walked over to his favorite place by a wild cherry tree, that he would no doubt someday be responsible to his Maker for allowing the Bird-of-Paradise tree to distract him, even when the peacock acted decorously.

In his letters home, he had often tried to describe the grace and beauty of the little tree, native to New Mexico gardens. Feathery branches lifting clusters of blossoms resembling golden birds with red aigrette top-knots had no doubt given rise to the name, and he regretted that his mother could not share with him the beauty of the one which stood by the south wall. Flowery birds, poised for flight, quivered in an occasional breeze idling on its way to raise little spirals of dust in the plaza beyond.

There, too, in direct line with his vision, were the hollyhocks standing straight and firm. Hardy and dependable always, they would soon be gone. His fondness for them was an impersonal one, because they always seemed a little stiff, never deviating from a detached friendliness as they guarded the outer gateway, bonnetted in red and white. Different, certainly, from the cosmas which had pushed themselves in riotous abandonment all along the pathway to form a right-about-face wall of pink and white loveliness the entire length of the portal.

As the autumn afternoon merged into evening, it seemed to have gathered up all the communal village noises and laid them gently aside, as if purposely providing a period of contemplation, and Father Docher saw, as he always did, the Creator of Heaven and Earth in the beauty of his garden. He always saw there, too, His power, in the varying seasonal texture of light by which strength was provided for the body, just as sanctifying grace was provided for the soul by prayer, discipline, and self-sacrifice. He had often longed for a closer, more intimate union with God, and a more complete realization of Him as manifested in the natural order; but realizing his limitations, he could only pray fervently to the Blessed Mother asking her to direct his friendly and jovial ways into the saints' paths of spirituality. Near the end of his long climb towards

The Padre of Isleta

spirituality, Father Docher was to be disciplined into the mold of contemplation, but on this afternoon he felt no premonition of the way by which the cross would come. He adjusted his prayer book several times in the fading afternoon light, sighed gently as he found it impossible to read in the approaching twilight, closed the book, and took out his rosary.

Neither the Office nor the rosary was said until late that night. The padre must have dozed off, he decided later, some place between an "Our Father" and a "Hail Mary," because he was startled into consciousness by the Angelus bells and a commotion in the plaza, not of Indian variety. Father Henri and Father Joubert arrived from the house in answer to his call just in time to join him in welcoming their Superior and friend, and a priest whom Archbishop Chapelle introduced as the new Vicar-General, Father Devereau.

Father Docher and his two compadres received with varying degrees of pride the congratulations of the Santa Fe guests on the beauty of the garden; the two compadres because they had contributed to the general effect by donations of flower seeds, slips of geraniums, or vines given to them, or begged by them, for the only missionary among the band scattered along the southern river valley who could make them grow.

As they passed Tina, still dumbly swinging on her perch, the padre of Isleta stopped with an introductory "Su Gracia" according to plans for a favorable impression, his feelings no doubt somewhat akin to those of St. Francis. But the feeling was only a matter of seconds. The Archbishop extended a friendly finger and murmured, "Buenos días." And then soldier, veteran of French-Colonial wars in far-off Cochin-China, peace-maker of Indians, went down in defeat before an onslaught of profanity which split the mystical beauty of the day into a thousand fragments of disgrace and mortification.

The peacocks and the birds on the Paradise Tree stood transfixed as the "Pride of Isleta" hurled oath after oath in bi-lingual profusion at all the brethren-in-Christ, but particularly at the saintly Chapelle.

When her fury had finally spent itself in one last triumphant leer, the distinguished prelate turned to his host and with the most polished of bows said, "Father, I don't believe that you are as successful

Archbishop Chapelle Is Welcomed

with birds as you are with Indians." And Father Docher, without stopping to pick up a single fragment of his love for Tina, returned the bow and led the way into the house.

16

Charles Fletcher Lummis Returns to Isleta

AT THE general store and post-office, the padre heard the amazing news that Charles Lummis had returned to Isleta. "And he is blind, totally so," continued Father Docher's good friend, George Seis, as he tied up the sack of sugar-cookies which the priest customarily "kept on hand" as a treat for the village children when they dropped in for a visit.

"Blind," repeated the padre, as he stuffed his other purchase, a blue bandana, in his coat pocket . . . *"Mon dieu."*

"They, say he had some kind of a fever in Guatemala, and that it left him that way. Thinks that he will recover his sight in this high altitude. Lord! I never heard of anyone coming to New Mexico for that kind of an ailment," drawled the expatriated New Yorker.

Father Docher's hurried "Adiós" included the postmaster-trader-merchant, and the day's prospective customers: Maria, staring at the bolts of calico with a calculating eye; Francisco, shifting his gaze from the buckets of lard to pink silk shirts; Pepita, slowly moving her tongue and a penny back and forth on the showcase of licorice, jawbreakers and gumdrops.

Although in his hurry he had neglected to ask where Charles Lummis was staying, the padre skirted the edge of the village and in a few minutes was at the Abeita adobe, where he felt confident he would find the ethnologist. Pablo Abeita met him at the door and brought him into the room where their old friend sat on the floor beside Mrs. Abeita, helping her clean *frijoles*. His eyes were bandaged, and a red silk handkerchief was tied across the bandages, but expert fingers were quickly sorting beans from chaff.

"It is the padre," said the fine looking Indian. "He came as soon as he heard." Charles Lummis dropped a handful of beans, jumped up, brought his moccasined feet together and then raised his hand in the old ringing salute to *El Padre Sargento.*

Ad. F. Bandelier in 1891. Padre Docher and Bandelier were long time personal friends.

Charles Fletcher Lummis Returns to Isleta

"It has been a long time," said the padre, blowing his nose in an effort to hide his emotion.

"Twenty years," replied the old friend, extending both hands which the padre grasped. "And they tell me that you have a long grey beard, and are petitioning your old standby, St. Jude, 'dispenser of impossible favors,' for an automobile so that you can get to Los Lunas in ten minutes. Now, padre, that is no way to get a Ford. The thing to do is to petition Washington. Pablo is going to head the delegation. I have already appointed him."

"The same Charles Lummis! And I was worried for fear I should find you changed," chuckled the priest, as he sat down on a Navajo-covered bench, above which hung a fine old *Santo*—of San Isidro.

"Blind, and slightly wizened and wrinkled as you can see, but the Puritan tradition is still flourishing," boasted Lummis.

"Cotton Mather would be proud of the traditional reserve still so obvious," laughed Pablo as he stooped to pick up the scattered beans.

"Heavens! Pablo, your erudition astounds me. Where on earth did you meet up with New England. In St. Michæl's College? Or, perhaps, during one of your many Presidential interviews, you discussed the heritage of my ancestors."

"I wasted no time talking about superfluous matters, I assure you," retorted Pablo. "I talked about the water rights, and land claims for my people. We now have about 2,000 acres under cultivation."

"Good work, Pablo," exclaimed Lummis. "And did you ask the great ones in Washington how they happened to forget that your grandfather loaned the government $18,000 during the Civil War? That story is going to be in my next book."

"Well, don't forget to mention that President Grant got the money back for us," cautioned Pablo. "My grandfather only waited twelve years for it . . . And, while we are on the subject of books, Mr. Lummis—"

Father Docher stirred uneasily because he knew what was about to be said by the governor of Isleta; and Mrs. Abeita left the room because she too knew what her husband was going to say to their old friend. Very slowly, and in tones of tribal authority, came the indictment.

The Padre of Isleta

"My people resented the publication of some of the material in one of your recent books, *Pueblo Folk Tales*. They felt that you revealed too many things which are of concern only to us. As the padre knows, it took me a long time to convince them that no harm had been done, because the stories are about people long since dead."

"I collected those tales when you were away at school, Pablo. Old Patricio told me most of them." And then quickly came the words which Father Docher hoped the famous writer would say to the governor of Isleta: "I should have asked your advice before I published them. I'm sorry." Not a bit of the old self-opinionated banter which Charles Lummis had characteristically and immediately raised in any verbal skirmish of conflicting ideas, beliefs or theories was apparent on this occasion. It was hidden away under a sincere cloak of apology, slightly tinged with fear.

"It was brought out in the meeting that Patricio had talked too much. It was a good thing that he died before the book was printed," commented Pablo. "But," and here the tribal tone of authority shaded and then blended into the old familiar pattern of friendship, "the very fact that I have received you as a guest in my home is proof that we have forgiven you. It was an act of indiscretion. We well consider the matter closed."

The tension in the little white-washed room, where Charles Fletcher Lummis had done much of his writing, was broken by the appearance of Mrs. Abeita with hot coffee, which the guest of honor drank with such audible enjoyment that the others looked at him in surprise. The padre decided that such an unusual display of gulping was merely a defense gesture for lifting the sophisticated man over a difficult barrier. But he knew, and the governor knew, that Charles Lummis' genuine love and respect for the people of Isleta had never been questioned at any time, in spite of the "indiscretion" committed.

"I came for first-hand news of you," said Father Docher. "Tell us everything. Pablo saw your picture in a paper once."

So "the returned one" began to talk. With sweeping strokes of a master craftsman, he took his two compadres on a magic journey of achievement and accomplishment. Highlighted on the bridge of time against a background of work-crowded years, moved the ethnologist, historian, folk-lorist and poet. Journeying with him, at times they saw the other old friend of bygone days, Adolphe Bandelier,

Charles Fletcher Lummis Returns to Isleta

raised to proportions of lasting eminence by the scientific world, and presented from the perspective of sincere admiration by his fellow worker.

It was not difficult for the priest, or the governor of the pueblo, to visualize the two men, Bandelier and Lummis, hiking hundreds of miles through Peru and Bolivia on the expedition which took them from New Mexico so long ago. Adolphe Bandelier armed with a transit and a bundle of notes. Charles Lummis with a forty-pound camera on his back, photographing everything of interest. For, as Father Docher later said, it was the same thrilling drama which they had seen enacted so many times with their own environment as the historical backdrop. The scene had merely shifted to South America. The "props" remained the same, the principal characters remained the same, the motivation remained the same. Two scholars searching for truth and knowledge, unmindful of bodily discomfort —of physical ailment.

To "see" Charles Lummis in the busy city of Los Angeles following his two-year archæological expedition to South America was a more difficult imaginative process. When Pablo said, "It is hard to picture you dressed in white man's clothes, with the white man's collar and shoes on," the padre nodded. Difficult it was, too, for them to keep up with the tabulated activities which the little man was checking off on his fingers, pausing significantly on each finger. Librarian of the Los Angeles Public Library for five years— founder and editor of *Land of Sunshine*—founder and editor of the "Landmark Club"—founder of the Southwest Museum.

"I have a new hobby, too," Lummis continued, as he cut the impressive, silent tribute to his great achievements with a depreciative hand-flip. "I have been making phonograph records of Spanish and Indian songs. Hundreds of them."

"The Guatemalan Expedition was the temporary undoing of me though," he sighed as he adjusted the red scarf over his eyes. "Had a bad case of jungle fever; hard luck that it should have left me this way. I just got a divorce, too. I guess that wasn't such hard luck though. But, I had better not go into my domestic difficulties; I might bore the padre." The bandage slipped again and, as Pablo got up to fix it for him, the news-bulletins continued.

"Queer, isn't it, that Adolphe Bandelier had trouble with his

The Padre of Isleta

eyes? Cataracts." ... "Cataracts? Mr. Bandelier had cataracts too?" the padre heard himself saying. But his voice seemed to be coming from a long ways off, weighted with some sort of a terrifying substance.

"What do you mean 'too,' padre?" inquired Lummis. "I haven't got cataracts. I thought I told you the cause of my blindness."

But the padre remained silent. Some other time, but not now—no, not yet ... would he mention the fact that the time was not far off when his own sight would be totally obscured by cataracts ... The vision in one eye was still quite good ... of course, he couldn't read very well—the letters blurred so—but he was still able to attend to his duties, and until the time came when he couldn't—no, he wouldn't say anything about it to Mr. Lummis ... no, not yet ... Anyway, the old friend was hurrying on with further news of Adolphe Bandelier, so there was no need now for answering the question.

"His second wife," continued Lummis, "was a great comfort to him during that trying time. She was his 'eyes' when his failed." The padre decided that there was something the matter with his ears when he heard those words, until Mr. Lummis added, as an afterthought, "Adolphe's first wife died, padre. He has always been a conventional man. You will never have to worry about him. Now, I—but I have done enough talking about myself. Let's talk about you. What have you been doing all these years?"

"The same thing that I was doing when you left, Mr. Lummis."

"Oh, I don't mean preaching the word of God to the people of Isleta, Peralta and Los Lunas. I mean interesting things. Haven't you anything to report besides missionary work? Heavens!"

The padre concentrated. He added and subtracted time. He sifted the years while Pablo Abeita watched and Charles Lummis waited, once ... twice ... three times ... and then he made his report. A tourist had given him some peacocks for his garden ... A friend from Valencia County had given him a new buggy ... Twice he had been to Santa Fe ... once to Las Vegas."

"Is that all?"

"That is about all, Mr. Lummis."

The scholar rose in order to pass judgment on the years which Father Docher had spread before him.

Pablo watched, and the missionary waited ... But the words were never said. From the plaza came the sound of the *tombe,* and the traditional call, *"mah-ee-kah; . . . Mah-ee-kah."* Then from all directions came the answering cry of the Indian boys on their way to the *estufa* for the Council Meeting. Pablo and the priest rose, and the three men listened in silence as the drum sounded the age-old message of duty. Charles Lummis smiled, and then said, as he slowly extended his hand towards Father Docher, "There is only one 'call' I don't understand. Your kind of a 'call,' Padre." The priest put the outstretched hand through his own arm, Pablo took the other arm of the blind scholar, and they guided him out for a walk around the plaza.

"I am off to the Jemez country tomorrow," Mr. Lummis said, as the drumbeats sounded louder and more insistent. "I want to investigate the Soda Dam up there. It has always interested me." And then, sensing the unasked question, he went on. "I am taking my son Quimi with me. He will be my 'eyes' . . . So—I guess it is, *hasta . . . la vista . . .* padre."

As Father Docher walked slowly over to the church "to make a little visit," his thoughts lingered sadly over that old farewell—"Until-I-see-you-again . . ."

17

The King and Queen of Belgium Visit Isleta

IT WAS the month of the brown and yellow moon, and the cottonwoods seemed covered with clustered golden butterflies that trembled and poised for an instant and then fluttered to the ground. The scrub-oak back from the river flared red.

The current of life in the village rushed stronger. It eddied and whirled in a maelstrom of preparation for a fiesta. It was not a fiesta for themselves. This was to be a fiesta for the friends of the people of Isleta. For a great chief was coming from across the waters. Father Docher had told them that this man was from his world and spoke his language. And now, in October, the people were to honor him.

For days they had prepared for this day. Sheep had been killed to provide mutton. Rabbits had been trussed to look-like-people and were roasting on fires. The people from Laguna had arrived the night before, bringing their drums for the dances, to dance with those of Isleta. To the north of the village were encamped cowboys from surrounding ranches. They were to contribute to the general entertainment by trick riding—a rodeo by the best on the range.

In the plaza of the village itself booths had been erected in each corner and covered with green of the spruce and cedar boughs. Now, in the early morning light, the people were hanging their blankets over the booths. Old blankets, with colors of red and black merging into softness of line from age, were proudly displayed, showing the wealth of families. A high-built coop of a spring wagon jostled over the road from Albuquerque. Its driver guided the horses to the southeast corner of the plaza. Then he began unpacking the wares of civilization—popcorn, hotdogs and pink soda pop. It was to be a great fiesta.

The King and Queen of Belgium Visit Isleta

In front of her house on the south side of the plaza, Maria arranged her pottery. She, the most expert pottery maker in the village, carefully placed bowls and ash trays moulded like birds, on a bench where the crowd could see them and buy them. And perhaps, by chance, the royal visitors would stop and admire them. Maria was the friend of rulers. Had not she made a visit to Washington with a delegation from Isleta to visit the Great White Father? And had not she shaken hands with the Great White Father Taft? There was a framed picture, commemorating the event, hanging in her front room. She stood back looking appraisingly at the bowls and ash trays. The people from Laguna would see that she had learned their art well, as was befitting the wife of a Laguna man. For there was little art left in the making of pottery among the people of Isleta.

Father Docher stepped into the patio in the early dawn and looked to the east. He saw that tips of the Manzanos were flushing pink in the paling grey of darkness. The sharp, cold freshness of autumn whipped his face and stung his nostrils. Over the wall of his patio came the sound of preparation for the program of the day.

All night the padre had thought of this day that was just now breaking—the day when the King and the Queen of the Belgians were to visit the pueblo of Isleta and worship with him in his church. The touch of the old world was sweet to him after his years of service in the new. Through the night the clump of the horses and the turn of their hooves on the gravel, as they passed on the path to the river, seemed a beat to the monotone of his memories. Now, he saw the dawn lighting his garden and the massed chrysanthemums turning slowly yellow.

In the early forenoon, he walked out and mingled with the people in the plaza. The church shone white and the windows were polished. Everyone had labored that hospitality be apparent to the white man, for this was the only time in the history of their remembrance that the priest had asked them to welcome his guests. A tiny boy stopped at his feet. "Look, Tashide, a penny. Those visitors there, they give him to me for dancing." And he bent and beat a few steps on the ground and then let out a whoop. The priest and the boy chuckled together in understanding. For they both knew the white men were child-like and simple, and believed anything the Indians told them.

The Padre of Isleta

The people waited, watching the sun "walking" through the sky. In the "straight-up" time of afternoon, the visitors arrived in the village. Hundreds of cars made a black line in front of the white houses in the plaza. A blue limousine stopped in front of the church. Out of it stepped a tall man, with shoulders erect, in the uniform of a Lieutenant-General of the Belgian army. Blue eyes swept the colorful crowd, and a stern mouth relaxed in a smile under the close-cropped moustache . . . King Albert I of Belgium turned to assist his Queen, Elizabeth, to step to the earth, packed hard by moccasined feet. The Crown Prince, Leopold, tall, young, eager, joined them. They looked in wonder at the whiteness of the houses reflected in the bright rays of the sun; at the mass of bright-blanketed people sitting in stolid stillness on the housetops; at the evergreen booths. And then, in the hush of the moment, came a shrill treble from their feet, "Look, lay-dee, give me a penny, I dance the Indian war dance," and royalty smiled at the earnest face of the youngster, and the sound of laughter rippled around the housetops like a spring wind in the corn leaves.

Age-old bells, the gift of a Spanish King to the Indian people, rang and the door of the mission church opened. Father Docher stood there in his cassock and surplice. He extended his hand to greet the most democratic of royalty, and expressed in French his welcome. He led them through the church, and into the sanctuary and the people of Isleta stood back to let their white visitors enter, and then crowded into the rear of the church and into the choir loft. All knelt for the prayers which Father Docher offered in a voice deep with emotion. He blessed them, and the King rose and placed on the priest's robe the emblem of the Belgian Order of Leopold. So a Belgian King honored a French missionary in a church of faith for the Indians.

In silence the people, with the King and the Queen, turned back to the plaza to witness the dances and the riding. As the plaza filled and packed there came a call from above them. On the south side stood an Indian crier on a rooftop. He lifted his arms for silence. Was this the official welcome to the village? Then rolled out in a mighty voice the words of the Indian herald. And the governor of the village translated the words to the visitors.

Since it was the month of the brown and yellow moon, the cattle

Padre Docher proudly wearing medals given to him by Leopold of Belgium on the occasion of his visit to Isleta.

The King and Queen of Belgium Visit Isleta

and horses were entered in the corn fields to feed at certain times together. But they were permitted to do this only at ten-day intervals. Some of the stock were straying; some were in the wrong fields. The next ones caught were to be put in the pound—confiscated.

So were the people warned, for seldom were so many together. Royalty, realizing the vital needs of life in a primitive village, smiled understandingly.

18

St. Rosalie

THE padre came out of the little confessional box at the rear of the church late one November afternoon. Although the women and children usually came to confession between two and five, the men, busy about the village, were often late. While waiting, the priest walked up the aisle of the church and sat down in the front row. His beard, which was grey now, he brushed absently aside, as he tilted his head to the right to peer at a painting. The peering disturbed him, but he accepted his failing eyesight as an act of time. A wealthy tourist from Tulsa had offered to pay the expenses to any oculist in the United States or in England, if he would go for a consultation, but as there was always something in the village to claim him, he had never bothered to have the trouble corrected.

Still there was joy to him in looking at the paintings, for with the exception of two, he had collected them for the church, one by one. Now this church in Isleta contained valuable works of art, as did many of the other Indian churches in the Rio Grande Valley. He remembered amusedly an article in a recent Art Magazine in which a connoisseur of art speculated rather plaintively in print about the fact that the works of old masters were frequently to be found in the primitive country of the Indians.

That long, narrow painting hanging to the left of the entrance into the sanctuary was undoubtedly one of the masterpieces. Shortly after he had come to Isleta, a trader had passed through the village carrying a pack on his back filled with thread, with needles, with cloth and, strangest of all, this painting. Father Docher had admired it. To him it expressed the suffering of man through the ages. But as usual money was lacking and he could not buy it.

On his return journey through the village, the trader walked into

St. Rosalie

the church one morning. He propped the picture against the chancel railing.

"Here, Father, take this picture. Hang it up in your church for your Indians. No one will buy the thing. I have carried it up and down the Rio Grande Valley until it feels like the 'old man of the sea' to my back. No. No money. Sometime at your devotions offer up a good Christian prayer for me, a Jew."

So, in such a way the picture had been added to the church. Father Docher was no art connoisseur, but he knew that Father Stoffel of Magdalena could give him something of the background. Father Stoffel on his new visit was entranced with the picture, for he was both a student and an art critic. After long examination of the picture, he came to the conclusion that "The Christ of Isleta" was a *retablo*, a fine example of Western Renaissance of the latter part of the Sixteenth Century. As Father Stoffel explained, a *retablo* was a picture of some sacred subject painted on the wall or suspended in a frame back of the altar.

It was of Gothic origin and had its beginning in ecclesiastical art during the Thirteenth Century. In the beginning it was but a rectangular piece placed behind the altar. Lateral panels were added in time. The Christ, garbed in a robe of woolen cloth, seemed wavering and faltering, yet the face was lighted with a spiritual calm which contrasted with the angular shape of the body. The fingers of delicate texture, the barren hill, the drapery, which separated the figure from all earthly objects, seemed to date the picture as of either the Flemish school of the Fifteenth Century or as an English copy of the Sixteenth Century. During the troubles of Elizabeth, many valuable works of the church had been spirited from England. And to Father Stoffel it seemed possible and probable that this was one of them.

Another painting that always fascinated Father Docher was "Our Lady of Guadalupe"—the Mexican saint with the square face and the calm, unquestioning gaze of one who had grown from the heart of the earth. Some forgotten friar in the days of the first conquest had chosen as a model a girl from one of the tribes of Mexico. Undoubtedly the people had brought "Our Lady of Guadalupe" back to Isleta when they had returned from the flight to the South after the rebellion of 1680.

The Padre of Isleta

Father Docher turned to another picture, "St. Rosalie." This hung above the entrance from the sacristy. It was obviously a picture by a Spanish painter, or possibly a copy of one done by an early friar. St. Rosalie's brown eyes stared from an oval Spanish face haughtily across the chancel at her Mexican sister. For some reason the Indians always preferred St. Rosalie. The padre's musings over the pictures were interrupted by the sound of the heavy front door opening, and the whisper of moccasined feet down the aisle. Rosalie, an Indian girl, stood before him, holding her blanket around her shoulders.

"Tashide, please, may we have St. Rosalie. She has been kind to me this year, and since I am named for her, we will give her a fine *velorio*. This day is my birthday, and we will have a big celebration." Here was the same old request, the one the Indians always made, and as he rose to take the picture from the wall, he noted again that St. Rosalie was fading, even as mortal woman fades when the years bear down upon her. The colors were dimming and the paint was checking. It didn't seem to be a question of age softening the colors. St. Rosalie was fading from other causes.

"Tashide," Rosalie turned a moment, "you come to *el velorio* tonight. We will welcome you."

So, at ten that night he went through the white stillness of the plaza. Black shadows from the houses bore down on the edges. As he walked he heard the murmur of voices. In front of the house of Ramon was a huge bonfire of cottonwood topped with cedar. The flames etched out the figures standing around in the gathering. Their cigarette tips circled back in the darkness. The men welcomed Father Docher with the friendliness of long understanding. One slipped back to the outer edge of the circle with a bottle of white fire. For, although Tashide did not scold long on the evils of drink, he definitely and completely forbade it to the people. The men talked of the hunt, and the young men chased and romped. One touched Father Docher, and as he circled around in the red light the priest tagged him as he passed again. The Indians laughed, for here was a priest who was as one of them.

In the house, the women were clustered around the fireplace. They were cooking rabbit meat, and frijoles, and chili. On the table was piled bread baked in the Spanish ovens, one of which stood

St. Rosalie

outside each house like a huge beehive. In the front room, St. Rosalie looked with impassive eyes over the gathering. A small table was loaded with the gifts—red beads, bright buttons, and calico of a hue to gladden the heart of the onlooker.

Such was the Indian *velorio*—a watch through the night, a celebration. *El velorio* of their Spanish neighbors meant a watch for the dead through the night until dawn. But this one for the Indian girl was simply a birthday party.

In the early morning the people crowded into the front room. Solemnly the girl named Rosalie walked over to the picture of St. Rosalie. She crossed herself, took the picture down, and placed it against the table. Her mother handed her a cloth and she dipped it into a bowl of warm water, rubbed the cloth carefully over a bar of lye soap. Before Father Docher realized the aim of the action, she scrubbed St. Rosalie thoroughly. Washing first her face with the lye soap made by the Indians, she then scrubbed the rest of the picture. Father Docher stepped forth to protest, then he dropped back in silence.

The next morning St. Rosalie was returned to the church. As the priest rehung the picture, he talked to the Indian girl watching. "That was a fine *velorio*," he ventured. Then, casually, "Why do you wash the Saint when all is over?"

The girl's eyes rounded in wonder at the very obvious question. But even Tashide, as long as he had been in Isleta, sometimes asked questions, the answers to which were certainly clear and simple.

"Has not Tashide taught us," she answered, "that we must bathe to be happy? That cleanliness is next to Godliness? Surely what is good for the people must be good for the Saints that hang in the sanctuary."

And St. Rosalie, the favorite, faded and worn from her baths, but undoubtedly clean in spirit, stared disdainfully at the Saint who was less God like.

19

Father Docher in St. Joseph's Hospital

THE dampness of the November snow came through the open window of the hospital room. Father Docher turned his head slightly to catch the stinging freshness of the air. He breathed deeply and his lips quirked into a smile, for the falling snow always brought back the memory of his first winter in New Mexico. That was—that was— he shook his head slightly ... was he really getting old? No, a man at seventy-six could hardly be called old, even though a hospital patient for three years. Of course, there was a birthday in two months now ... in January, 1929.

The things of his youth came back to him clearly. Thirty-seven years ago he had first ridden into Isleta in the early dusk of a December evening ... past the well by the church. The *Convento* dark. A thin silver light from below a door. His knock. A push on the door. An Indian woman, her shawl back on her shoulders, leaning over a stove stirring, a red wick glowing in an oil lamp. The woman's startled gaze and a muttered *"madre de Diós,"* as she crossed herself. "Father Padilla!"

Father Docher pulled the pillow under his head more comfortably. His fingers explored carefully the top of the enameled stand by his bed—slick, slippery, cool—there—a glass of water. The puckering dryness in his throat relieved, he turned his head again toward the window.

Father Padilla—may his soul rest in peace ... "The rising of the body is not a miracle. Either the change in the flow of the water which is near the surface in this valley forces that cottonwood coffin to the surface, or the seismical changes which are an undisputed fact of this country cause it." He could hear again the close clipped tones of the scientifically-minded padre, as the priests discussed the testimony of the Indians concerning the rising of the body of Father Padilla. Such a compact and neat disposal of the problem that was an integral part of the lives of the Isleta people! That assumption

Father Docher in St. Joseph's Hospital

had not been included in the report sent to the Archbishop, for certainly it was not direct evidence. But it was impossible to be so factual with Indians. Bandelier had taught him the primary fears of their life. That fear of the unknown. It wasn't only Indians who were afraid of the unknown. All men were. And the Indians always had a supernatural explanation for all they could not understand. How well Bandelier knew that. Bandelier, buried in far-off Spain . . . so far had his restless mind and restless feet carried him.

Father Docher dozed a little time. Or was it a long time? Time meant so little now. Shut in this world of darkness by the cataracts that he had never had time to have removed. A deep roaring sound disturbed him. The boat careened madly on the tops of the waves of the river. Early spring floods from the melting snows of the mountains. "Father?" It was Juan the boatman, who was trying to row the boat from the Isleta side to the east side, where El Laguna settlement was located, for no bridge then spanned the Rio Grande. "Father, is this hell?" Juan had asked. Father Docher had permitted a half smile. Why in the English language did the Indians invariably learn the outlawed words first.

"Hell? My son, I don't know. But I do know that if you don't handle this boat more carefully the two of us will soon know what hell is."

But the roaring sound wasn't from the river. It was only the roar in his own ears. His lips moved silently as he repeated the Ordinary of the Mass, for that offered him solace. Three years before, the Sovereign Pontiff at Rome had given him special dispensation, granting him the right to use the same Mass ritual each day instead of varying each day's ritual, as is required by the laws of the church.

The tap-tap of quick-moving feet on the linoleum in the hall. "Hello, Father. May I get you something? Your pipe, for instance?" The young freshness of a nurse's voice.

"Here's your pipe. Here's the tobacco. No woman can learn to tamp the tobacco in a pipe for a man. I'll shut this window. Oh! How do you do, Sister." The crisp swish of the starched habit of the Sister in charge. The eternal checking of the nurses as to duties, the eternal routine of hospital life. But bodies had to be saved as well as souls.

The clank of the crank at the foot of the bed. "I'll crank you up."

The Padre of Isleta

The marvel of the hospital beds ... how it eased his aching bones; and the pipe was drawing well. His fingers traveled again over the stand by his bed ... matches ... ash tray. Someone of the Isleta Indians would be in with gossip of the pueblo, or for a discussion of their Indian beliefs. Not that they discussed their beliefs with white men often. That Hopi, now. The one who had laid the stones in the ceremonial altar in the Harvey House here in Albuquerque. That was in 1910. And the Indian had died horribly. "Yes," the Indians had whispered, "he told the secrets of his tribe. He laid for the white man the altar as it is in their *kiva* and his tongue grew thick and black and hung from his mouth." Well, that was the way legends and traditions started; traditions that sometimes caused trouble too.

The time he had had in persuading the Isleta people to use the new burial ground to the southwest. For when he had gone to Isleta the plot of ground in front of the church was filled, literally to overflowing, with their dead. So well had they learned their lesson that graves must be in consecrated ground, that they refused to heed him when he suggested a new *Campo Santo*. Even when he had pointed out that the bones were visible when the wall on the east side of the church was moved, they answered with a characteristic shrug, "We have always used this." What a test to his patience that had been.

A high faint mew of a cat came to his ears. Or was it a peacock? Strange that they sounded alike at times. He would never forget the time an Indian had brought him two peacocks in an old Ford car, so that he would not be lonely in the hospital, and how hard put the Sisters had been in finding a place for them. Not wanting to disappoint his Indian friend, he had pointed out gently that a hospital room was, after all, hardly the place for peacocks, beautiful though they might be. The Sister had finally solved the rather delicate question by arranging for a wire fence in the patio back of the hospital, and for a year two peacocks had strolled among the Sisters' flowers.

There was the slip of moccasined feet in the hall. "Why, Diego!" He would know the sound of Diego Abeita's walk anywhere. "All afternoon, Diego, I have lived in the past and now you bring me the present."

The rustle of the newspaper sounded as Diego pulled a chair to the side of the bed. "There is snow, Tashide. The people are plan-

Father Docher in St. Joseph's Hospital

ning a hunt in Eagle Feather Mountain." What was wrong? Diego sounded strained. Again the newspaper rattled.

"What do you have there, Diego? It sounds like a thick paper, a newspaper of many pages. Not like the papers of this city."

"It is a Los Angeles paper, Father. It concerns Lummis."

"Lummis. Now, what has he done?" Then into the silence a squeak from the chair as Diego moved uneasily. "Oh, I understand. He is dead."

"Yes, Tashide, and I thought you would want to hear of your friend . . . "

Bandelier, now Lummis . . . Men who were flushed with youth and a burning flame . . . analyzing . . . discussing in an Indian village in New Mexico their hopes, their future . . . Diego's voice verged into the musings . . .

"The Los Angeles *Times,* November 26, 1928."

"Read it, Diego, tell me what the paper says about my old friend, Lummis."

Carefully, in government Indian School English, Diego read the article.

"Dr. Charles Fletcher Lummis, author, poet, explorer and distinguished historian, died at 12:30 P. M., yesterday of cancer, in his sixty-ninth year. Hope for his life began to fade about two weeks ago, although Mr. Lummis knew last February that he suffered from an incurable malady, and cancer experts could promise him no more than another year of life.

"With this knowledge, Dr. Lummis decided that there was yet another achievement with which to round out his eventful life. He wished to complete his life's poems and publish them, and sheer strength of will bent him to the task. He worked at top speed, and with the aid of Harry Herbert Knibbs, prepared his manuscript and it was accepted on October 26th.

"Usually a book taken at this late date is published the following spring, but knowing Dr. Lummis' condition, his publishers hastened the work of bringing out the volume. This, *Bronco Pegasus,* his last work, was returned from the bindery on the eighth, and in order to get the book in to Dr. Lummis' hands before his eyesight failed, a copy was sent to him by airmail.

"It was after his arrival here, and during the two years from

The Padre of Isleta

1885 to 1887 when he served as city editor of the *Times* that Mr. Lummis first became devotedly interested in the history and customs of the Great Southwest, an interest which placed him in the coveted pre-eminent position as the state's foremost historian. For five years Lummis lived among the Indians in Isleta Pueblo, N. M., where one of his daughters, Turbese, named by the Indians from the Rainbow, was born. His exploration trips carried him from Canada to Chile, and many of his study tours were made on horseback. His books on the history of Spanish America have become standard. For his research in this field he was knighted by the King of Spain in 1915. Since 1905 Mr. Lummis made phonograph records of 550 old Spanish songs of the Southwest, and 425 Indian songs in 37 languages.

"In 1912 he suffered an attack of blindness, the result of jungle fever contracted in Guatemala, where he had gone as a member of the executive committee of the Southwest Museum to direct the American Archæological expedition among the Mayan ruins. He recovered his eyesight in the rarified atmosphere of the mountains of New Mexico, where he had begun his explorations twenty-five years before."

"What else? Pablo. They must have said other things about him."

"There is another piece, Padre, and he would have liked it. It is called "High Tribute Paid to Friend,' by John Steven McGroarty. You will like it too. I will read it."

"If it was so ordained that when a man passed out of this life into spiritual world he would appear before the Gates of Paradise in the familiar guise by which he was known on earth, it would have been interesting to witness the arrival of Charles Fletcher Lummis at St. Peter's watch-tower yesterday when his blithe soul had taken wing upon the journey that leads beyond the tracery of the stars.

"The folk loitering on the high ramparts of heaven would have seen a little old fellow arrayed in corduroy, a red sash around his waist, a soft shirt and collar, a red cravat, and a cowboy Stetson banded with leather on his head; a little old fellow with a face tanned by sun and wind, his eyes deep and eager, a challenge on his lips.

"Mostly it would be the old pagans who would flock to greet him, for he was essentially one of them by reason of some strange throwback which made him so, although he was New England born and

Father Docher in St. Joseph's Hospital

bred, steeped in the pools of Pilgrim tradition at his birth. He was a pagan in the way that he resented conventions and that he lived his life in his own way. I often told him that he was lawless and so he was. Which is to say that as far as his own life was concerned he framed it to laws of his own. He had the courage to do it, as many of us have not. And if he is now, and ever was to be blamed for it, let us dwell upon the fact that if there are no pagans in heaven it must be because there is no such place.

"Not that he was without reverence for beliefs other than his own. I knew him well, and admired him tremendously. All of us who scribble at the history and tradition of California and the Southwest are indebted to him for inspiration. He was the master. No other man was so steeped in our lore, or had the embracing sympathy that he had for the things and the people who were here before we came.

"He will be missed in many quarters, and not the least where scholars foregather and among whom he sat palm-crowned. There were many who loved him and, after all, that's the best that any one can say above a dead man's pulseless clay. God rest his soul, and may peace be with him."

"Adolphe Bandelier, and now Charles Lummis," said the padre sadly, as Diego folded the paper . . . "and soon it will be Anton Docher . . ."

Diego could say nothing, for he too knew that the padre's strength could not withstand the complications of old age much longer. The doctors had told him that it was only a question of months . . .

"We will have quite a reunion when we all get together again. And we will be waiting for you, Diego," he added, as the Indian knelt by the bed for the blessing he felt might be a final one from the padre of Isleta.

20

History and Legend

ONE month later, on December 18, 1928, the body of Father Anton Docher lay in state before the altar in the Isleta Church. Bright blanketed Indians formed a guard of honor around the coffin of the priest who had served them for thirty-four years. All day and far into the night, young and old of the tribe filed past the bier to gaze for the last time on the face of him "who was one of us." Cold and still as the statues above were his features, but bright and colorful on the breast lay the French-African War medal and the Belgium Order of Leopold. Sharing the twenty-four hour watch were Spanish neighbors and Anglo friends from Los Lunas, Peralta and Los Padillas.

Clergymen in great numbers came for the Pontifical Funeral Mass sung by Archbishop Albert T. Daeger. After the funeral sermon preached by Father Dumarest of Las Vegas, eight Indians lifted the coffin to their shoulders, and the body of the *"padrecito"* was borne entirely around the plaza he had loved. As the bearers re-entered the church, the Office for the Dead was chanted by the religious orders. Bright sun-swords flecked from the high windows on the east and filtered past Franciscan friars, Dominican monks, black-robed Sisters of Charity, a tapestry of medieval design in a pueblo setting. Then the body of Father Docher was buried in front of the altar, by the side of Father Padilla.

And, as time flows on, the people of Isleta tell their children the stories of their own people handed down from generation to generation orally. As they tell the legend of Father Padilla, they always tell what has now become another legend. How Father Docher examined the remains of Father Padilla on that day in April when the churchmen gathered and exhumed the body. They say that with his own hands he found the wound that had caused the death of the

History and Legend

early churchman and white worms were there, one of which bit him. But the realists say that he ran a splinter of bone in his finger, which became infected. Then his hand and arm became swollen, and black to the shoulder. Days passed for Father Docher in a red veil of suffering. The doctors said that the arm must come off—either that, or death was certain. And the padre had thought of the power of the faith he taught—surely prayer would help him in his affliction, and he knelt before the altar and promised a *novena* of Masses each year for Father Padilla if the infection would leave him. And the purple swelling and the blackness of the priest's arm did recede, and he grew well and strong again. Surely here, they say, was a miracle, an answer to prayer and believing. Every year thereafter, Father Docher celebrated the Masses of Thanksgiving in gratitude to the Martyr-priest for his help in time of trouble.

Neither priest, the people of Isleta always add when telling this story, will ever be forgotten. Both are a part of their history, of their traditions, of their legends.

THE END

www.ingramcontent.com/pod-product-compliance
Lightning Source LLC
Chambersburg PA
CBHW022106160426
43198CB00008B/369